Testimonials

Dysfunction Interrupted sh.... .... ted my thinking patterns and m..... .... s just going to be depressed and anx..... j..ever. I now feel better and have enthusiasm for my future. **—Teresa M.**

Dr. Sherman was very responsive to emails and questions regarding program. I never felt alone working through my problems. Very helpful and knowledgeable in her field. **—Ruth P.**

I never understood why I felt so scared all the time and couldn't focus on anything. Dysfunction Interrupted gave me answers to these problems and tools I could use to feel better. **—George B.**

Great program! Informative and helpful as I had suffered for years with anxiety as well as depression and nothing was working. I now feel good most days and am able to easily get through the days that aren't so great. **—Nancy M.**

Dysfunction Interrupted was the best thing to ever happen to me! I had been in one bad relationship after another and could never understand why things didn't work out. I would go from bad to worse and I became very depressed, ready to give up on ever finding someone and ready to spend the rest of my life alone. Dr. Sherman coached me through the program step-by-step and we worked out the "skeletons" that were keeping me from finding love. I feel better than ever about myself and ready to face the dating world without fear of another disaster. **—Kathryn S.**

I not only feel better, I have now put in place a life that I want and look forward to getting up each day. **—Bob B.**

After years of taking antidepressant medications and going to therapist after therapist to find relief from depression that started as a teen I am now medication free and enjoying my life as I believe I was meant to. Dr. Sherman and her program taught me what I needed to get out of this rut and I am eternally grateful. I highly recommend the program and Dr. Sherman. **—Debbie G.**

I worked through the Dysfunction Interrupted *program with Dr. Sherman as my coach. I can't believe the gains I made in such a short time in my career, not to mention my personal life. I had been stuck in a career I hated and in a relationship that was going nowhere. I look forward to every day for the first time ever and hold hope that my new skills will continue to bring me new and exciting experiences.* **—Darlene F.**

Dr. Sherman took me through her program and uncovered at every turn the things that I had learned that were causing me to lead a life full of bad choices. I had really good parents, but some of their habits and ideas that weren't very productive had rubbed off on me and I was recreating their problems in my own life. Dysfunction Interrupted *allowed me to learn new thinking skills and gave me a tool box for life that has brought many happy moments instead of regret. I wish I had found this sooner.* **—Patricia M.**

Dysfunction Inter rupted®

How to Quickly Overcome Depression, Anxiety and Anger Starting Now

Audrey Sherman, PhD

CONCORD PUBLISHING

Dysfunction Interrupted®
Audrey Sherman, PhD

© 2015 Audrey Sherman
All rights reserved.

DISCLAIMER
The information provided within *Dysfunction Interrupted* is designed to provide
helpful information on the subjects discussed. It is not meant to be used,
nor should it be used, to diagnose or treat any psychological or medical condition
or to render any type of psychological, medical, legal or other professional advice.
For diagnosis or treatment of any psychological or medical problem, consult your own
physician. The publisher and author are not responsible for any specific health concern
that may require medical supervision and are not liable for any damages or negative
consequences from any treatment, action, application or inaction by or to any person
reading or following the information in this book. No warranties or guarantees are expressed
or implied by the author or publisher. Neither the publisher nor the author shall be liable
for any physical, psychological, emotional, financial or commercial damages including,
but not limited to, special, incidental, consequential or other damages. The reader is
responsible for his or her own choices, actions, and results. References are provided for
informational purposes only and do not constitute endorsement of any
websites or other sources.

Cover + Interior design: Rebecca Finkel, F + P Graphic Design
Publisher: Concord Publishing, Naples, Florida
Book Consultant: Judith Briles, The Book Shepherd

Library of Congress Catalog Number: 2015910842
ISBN: 978-0-9861534-0-2
ebook ISBN: 978-0-9861534-1-9

Categories for cataloging and shelving:
1. Self-help   2. Psychology   3. Mental Health

10   9   8   7   6   5   4   3   2   1

Printed in USA

Reminded

Yesterday I was reminded
about certain things of my past
Sometimes I wonder how I changed my direction
as time went by so fast.

My family didn't seem dysfunctional
it seemed as normal as could be
Maybe there were things I was missing
things I was just too young to see.

Sometimes I am reminded
of things I went through
It reminds me of the pain I had to endure
as there was nothing else I could do.

Even though I remember
just as if it were yesterday
I certainly hold no grudges
toward anyone in any way.

The way I see it
things were the way they were supposed to be
I grew up with hardship
but it made a man out of me.

It was a voice from the past
that shined light on my earlier years
There were some very dark times
and certainly many fears.

Happy and somewhat content
in these days as I grow old
I continue writing my poetry
with much wisdom to me told.

Dysfunction Interrupted is dedicated

to all my clients through the years.

By sharing your lives and difficulties,

you inspired and motivated me

to write down what I thought

everyone should know.

Contents

Introduction

"Life can only be understood backwards;
but it must be lived forwards."
—SOREN KIERKEGAARD

Do you engage in self-destructive behavior?

Do you have a hard time making decisions?

Do you get angry all the time?

Do you lack self-confidence?

Do you experience trouble when trying to focus?

Do you suffer from chronic depression and/or anxiety?

Do you have ongoing relationship difficulties
or are you coming out of a destructive relationship?

If you have answered "yes" to any of these questions, you are in the right place. Wouldn't you like to put these issues to rest and experience joy in your life? Are you tired of carrying around heavy loads of emotional baggage? Wouldn't you like to feel in control of yourself and your life?

Dysfunction Interrupted® has been written with all this in mind. It covers everything you need to know in order to address these issues and move ahead in life.

Based on my two decades in clinical practice as a psychologist using Cognitive, Developmental and Positive Psychology, my goal is to reach the scores of individuals suffering from dysfunctional pasts and the ongoing emotional difficulties that can result. *Dysfunction Interrupted* is derived from witnessing clients who were dealing with unfortunate or even mildly dysfunctional pasts that had kept them stuck in destructive or non-productive thought patterns. Interestingly, I also found that sometimes the patterns were not a product of dysfunction in the developmental years at all, but rather

> **The good news is that there are only so many things that can go wrong with a person due to less than ideal or even abusive parenting.**

a simple lack of information provided by caregivers. Caregivers that lacked basic tools that would have supported their children's development and behaviors.

The patterns and habits learned and then employed daily in your thought processes and interactions with others are often the culprits that keep you unhappy. They keep you saddened, not reaching out for your goals, not feeling worthy of happiness, and not relating to others as you would like. Those patterns and habits keep you from enjoying healthy bonds with good friends and choosing partners who are good for you. They even keep you afraid when there is nothing to be afraid of and sad for reasons you don't understand.

If you have children, these same patterns keep you struggling to raise them and wondering why that might not be working out very well. Worst of all, as you struggle day-to-day with depression and fear and unhealthy relationships, you don't have time to enjoy the life you have or don't take time to create the life you would like to have because you think it is either not possible or you don't deserve it. You may even have been told by someone in your life that you were "destined to fail" or "won't amount to anything."

If you have been struggling with emotional issues for a while, it's likely that you have been told by someone to "think differently." That message is incomplete, especially if you're not motivated to change or don't understand why your thinking is the way it is. Being told to "think differently" often makes you defensive; you feel you are being criticized. In fact, it only reinforces old thought patterns; you want to dig in your heels. Instead, identifying the exact way you were trained to think and react and then unlearning the negative aspects is the key to being able to think and behave differently.

Believe it or not, a lot of the symptoms that are giving you trouble today are the normal reactions of a healthy brain to unfortunate circumstances. Anxiety is normal in the face of chaos or even danger—not a disorder. Depression and shutting down in the face of chaos with no strategy for relief is also a normal process. So anxiety or depression or both are letting you know something needs an overhaul in your life. It is time to take control.

My experience shows that understanding the difference between a disorder and a learned pattern is encouraging and instills hope in a person. Through the years, I have worked with clients who have been to a variety of psychologists and other professionals. They were labeled negatively for what is a perfectly normal reaction. Eliminating or relearning something is far more hopeful and positive than feeling like you have a disorder you can never overcome. The intent of *Dysfunction Interrupted* is to identify the symptoms, identify their origins, and eliminate them or at least help you to gain control.

These "symptoms" all have names such as depression, anxiety, etc., and all can be worked on with amazing results.

I have studied and utilized the self-help resources available as a therapist for years, using them for my client practice. Not surprisingly, a need for a shorter, "how to" type of program that is clearly presented, comprehensive and provides hope along with long-lasting results was needed. As I researched other programs and books, I thought to myself, "How could I make this easier and quicker in this busy world?" In your hands is the result—*Dysfunction Interrupted*. It has been designed to encompass and provide strategies for all parts of your life. You will quickly be replacing things that are not working and begin to feel happiness and control over your destiny. If you follow this program and implement the techniques and strategies, you will feel better immediately.

Motivation is critical to your success. Are you tired of feeling bad? To benefit fully from what I will propose within the Dysfunction Interrupted program, you:

- Must desire to feel some joy and want to move beyond past hurts and disappointment.
- Must take responsibility for your well-being, even if it is hard work from where you are starting; and
- Must dedicate some time to work on it and decide to not give up.

This is not to say that you will feel like a million dollars every day of your life—no one does. But using *Dysfunction Interrupted* will give you purpose and add joy and control to what might otherwise feel like an out-of-control life.

Dysfunction Interrupted is a guide and reference that tells you what to do or how and where to seek what you need. If you commit to doing the things suggested in this book and program, your life will improve more quickly than you can imagine. The websites and resources that I recommend have been evaluated applying my criteria of being straightforward, user friendly and cost-effective. As a subscriber to the resources I recommend, I have utilized the products and programs before sharing them with you.

This program is not designed to blame, punish or negate your parents in any way. Instead it describes the developmental processes that most likely led to the current dysfunction. Some parents do the best they can, others don't; some are clueless to parenting skills and others don't even try; some only repeat what they know and don't bother to see if it is healthy for their children or not—they figure they turned out all right so it must be okay; some individuals are very sick themselves, and they really have no business raising children, but they do so anyway; and some love their children very much, yet have no idea how to parent and just kind of "wing it."

The good news is that there are only so many things that can go wrong with a person due to less than ideal or even abusive parenting. This may seem like an impossible statement from where you are right now, but I assure you that it is true. It just feels like there must be more because of how overwhelming the symptoms can be for you and how they permeate your entire life. That overwhelm may feel so immense that your attitude becomes: Why should I even bother to try to change?

If you suffer from anxiety, depression, trauma or worse, you are most likely not sure what to do about it or how to handle it. All of this impacts your personal, work, parenting and relationship life today. The good news is that the web you are caught in is not permanent— it's never too late to get on track. Age does not matter here.

There are a few forms of genetically and medically related conditions that can cause depression and anxiety including thyroid difficulties,

diabetes and other endocrine problems and brain injury. Contrary
to what many espouse, I do not believe that these account for the
enormous increase we have seen in the past two decades in emotional
problems. Nor do I buy into the disease theory of life as the daily
media delivers through commercials and infomercials that pepper
the airwaves. There are no conclusive studies that prove this to be
the case. It makes for great lifetime customers of drug companies,
but not for a satisfactory and pleasant life.

The bottom line is, even if you suffer from a medical condition that
affects your moods, you can learn the skills necessary to feel the
best that you can under the circumstances. Why suffer more than
you have to?

Most maladaptive behaviors and thought patterns stem from
learned behaviors that our parents modeled or were reactions
to unhealthy environments. If you grew up never feeling good
enough, then of course you will be depressed. That is a normal
reaction, not abnormal. If you grew up frightened for the safety of
yourself, your siblings and/or the other parent, then you of course
are going to be an anxious sort. That is the way the brain works.
And, be thankful your brain works, that is the first step here to
change. This book delves into the processes and enables you to
decide what went wrong and when.

It may be upsetting to think about some of these things again, but
remember we are not staying there for long—just long enough to
determine where you go now. We have to determine your starting
point to map out your end point. You can now choose your path
and your lifestyle. What you think is normal may not be at all, and
the heaviness of living that way can be lifted.

Along with eliminating the negativity comes the outcome: building a great life. Otherwise, a void is left that without new skills will

simply fill back up with the old set of skills that were not working very well in the first place. After all, if you already knew how to build a better life, you would have done so. If you knew how to grasp opportunities and make them work for you, you would have.

> **There are simple answers to why things are as they are—all you need is that information.**

This does not have to be difficult. Facing years of therapy, rehashing the past over and over is not the answer. It's the methodology of yesteryear that fails in too many cases. There really are simple answers to why things are as they are—all you need is that information. My desire is to help you:

- understand your personal challenges;

- master them to the point where they are not holding you back;

- eliminate them altogether by using the *Dysfunction Interrupted* nine steps of the program;

- build a happy and satisfying life.

I have designed this to be as painless and quick as possible, so as to not waste your time. Working through long self-help books can be depressing in and of itself. Reading about the misery of others definitely does not resolve anything for you or move you forward.

Dysfunction Interrupted is designed to identify what's holding you back. Each section is just as important as the next; don't skip around. Please follow the text in the order presented. Although you may feel that certain sections do not pertain to you, read them anyway. They might relate to someone close to you and the information will give you greater insight into that person's psyche.

Part I of the program examines the major family patterns that can lead to emotional difficulty and dysfunction. It explains how negative reactions develop in a person's experience. Along with each family pattern are the typical types of ongoing dysfunction one might be experiencing due to that particular parenting style. The stories that open each pattern are true with names changed.

Part II defines these symptoms or difficulties so that you can determine which apply to you. It gives more in-depth explanations of each problem area and allows you to see how the symptoms may all be connected, and not separate issues.

Part III covers the nine steps or skill bases that you will learn to master in order to eliminate your difficulties. Even if a step sounds like it doesn't apply to you, read the entire program so you can see how the steps are all intertwined. Give each idea a try, even if it sounds like the most ridiculous thing you have ever heard. Many changes to thinking happen only after actual behavior has changed and better or different results are experienced. Don't rely on "feeling like doing it someday" as that day may never come.

The 9 Steps

1. Self-Soothing applies to all problems and is a key skill to master.

2. Cognitive-Based Work teaches you to use your thoughts to your advantage and to place yourself in a better frame of mind; how to control your thoughts in order to master your life and your experience of life in general; discover where your old thought patterns (that you learned from your family) have hindered your progress so far; and learn new language skills and thought patterns that move you into a whole new and exciting world of experience.

3. Biofeedback provides a visual on the things learned in the previous two steps. Our thoughts produce a bodily counterpart. Doing biofeedback helps you to see this in real time and learn to control your thoughts in order to control your bodily responses.

This skill is fun and enlightening to use. It's especially effective for anyone who may suffer from panic and high anxiety.

4. The Advanced Thinking Skills build upon the previous three steps to move into a realm of life you never thought possible. You will learn the critical thinking skills of those who truly engage in and master life. This is the thinking of those who take from life all that they need to live full and productive lives, unburdened by depression, high anxiety, massive anger or any of the other problems you may face. You'll learn to emulate the truly successful in order to live a life of your creation and dreams.

5. Lose the Fear also builds on the previous skills learned. It addresses how to eliminate the fears that hold you back and keep you stuck in poor jobs, poor relationships, and poor anything else. You'll discover how fear is the number one limiting emotion you can experience. When you master your fears, you move full speed ahead into your newly designed and strategically planned life.

6. Boundary Setting & Relationship Overhaul is designed to help you investigate your relationships and how you are with the people in your world. You may need to perform a relationship overhaul with some of your close friends and/or family members, and this step is designed to give you the tools to do so. Setting boundaries is a simple concept yet something that's often overlooked as you manage your relationships. The goal here is to understand what boundaries are and how their usage is imperative in one's life design.

7. Enrichment teaches you how and why to fill your days with the things that actually make life worth living. By removing the focus on misery and pain, you will learn to concentrate on fun and enjoyment and the fulfillment of relationships and gratification. You cannot be miserable if you're having fun; it is impossible!

8. Body Basics contains information crucial to your overall mental health. What and how you feed your brain determines how it's going to work for you. This step provides resources and knowledge on how to get you in the best working condition possible.

9. Get It Together! is critical to overall functioning. This step provides you with tools to eliminate organizational and time-management difficulties. Armed with new tools, you will be able to avoid feeling that you are in complete chaos or are being over-whelmed. Such experiences, like overwhelm, make people just want to tune out of life. When you get it together, you free up the time necessary to add things to your life that you actually enjoy.

Appendix A is a list of resources for further exploration of the topics covered.

As you read the book and do the exercises, you may find that you need help or are really stuck on one topic. Our website *PsychSkills.com* is available for asking questions. In addition, **personal program coaching** is also available if you feel you require more attention and one-on-one time as you progress. **Teleclasses and seminars** will also be available on a regular basis, addressing each topic.

As you begin to move forward, know that *Dysfunction Interrupted* is designed to turn your life around and to give you hope and joy. Choose to use the tools that are the most helpful to you.

PART one

Major Patterns of Dysfunction in Families

"It is never too late to become what you might have been." —George Eliot

Many suffer from less than ideal thinking patterns, based on what they learned in their dysfunctional family of origin. These thinking patterns keep them stuck and less happy than they'd like to be: fear, anxiety and depression are the result. They may be afraid to hope for something better; consistently experience bad relationships; or make the wrong decisions and choices.

Does that ring true for you? If so, *Dysfunction Interrupted* has the answers and solutions.

Unsupportive and self-destructive thinking patterns can be difficult to rework. As a psychologist, I find that those who are the most successful in unraveling and reworking those patterns were able to find mentors or people who took them under their wing and taught them the things their own parents could not. Not everyone has had that opportunity until now. The *Dysfunction Interrupted* program strives to teach you the necessary skills to overcome the unproductive patterns. A new you will surface.

I'm not out to negate your parents or upbringing in any way. This is just to point out how their parenting behavior and the environment you grew up in may have caused you to develop some faulty thinking styles. Most likely, your parents were imitating their own parents or behaving in a way that was a reaction to their own parenting.

As you work through the *Dysfunction Interrupted* program, you may be able to identify some patterns in them that stemmed from their own childhoods. Don't panic and think that you will have to tell them off or cut them out of your life. This program is to *help you,* and not to create stress. I'm not going to ask that your parents go to therapy, or that you confront them in any way. Why? Usually I find this not to be very helpful and only results in opening old wounds. What is important is for you to understand the lasting effects their behavior may have had on you. This way, you can choose to correct it and devise your own life under your own thinking rules. You become in charge.

Of course, there are many parenting styles and combinations of family styles. However, I have found the following to be the most detrimental in terms of creating dysfunctional patterns that endure through time and generations. Keep in mind as you read through Part I that typically each of your parents also came from one or more of these styles and brought those characteristics to the parenting table. They were a product of two other sets of individuals and so on. Think of it as a domino effect.

It's not unusual to discover some thinking styles that are limiting without having to go very far back in your ancestry. Also, your parents' or grandparents' thoughts could have had a constructive function at some point in time. As you move through *Dysfunction Interrupted*, I encourage you to come to understand where the thinking patterns were established and consider whether they make sense in your life at this time.

In This Section

1

Violent and Directly Abusive Parents ... Meet "The Bullies"

"The past cannot be changed; the future is yet in your power." —UNKNOWN

Annie is an overweight, nervous, middle-aged woman with a nice smile who wants to please everyone. She has come to me for help with ongoing depression and anxiety that she reports has been with her as long as she can remember. She doesn't sleep well, has stomach upset and feels increasingly fatigued on a daily basis. She describes her marriage as "OK" but looks away from me as she says this. She owns a local hair salon and runs a successful business.

Her upbringing is like many—a middle class family in a suburban neighborhood. On the outside looking in, she had an ideal family life with many nice perks due to her father's career. Her mother was a stay at home mom and housewife, keeping everything running smoothly and tidily. The outside world was oblivious to the darker side. Her father wouldn't allow her mother to work— he liked having full control over her by keeping her financially dependent. An alcoholic, he was physically abusive to her mother, her brother and herself.

Annie's father would stop by a local hotel bar on the way home from work each day and have a couple of cocktails, declaring that he needed to entertain clients. His next stop was at another local watering hole for a couple more, this time without the clients. Upon arriving home, he would proceed to consume another several drinks over the course of the evening until such time as he fell into a stupor. It was the time between him arriving home and the stupor that was a nightmare for the family.

She revealed that he would become physically abusive at least three times a month, and the family was always on eggshells waiting for the outburst that would precede the violent episodes. They were not predictable in content, just that they were sure to happen with being angry over something at work as the precursor. His violent repertoire included turning over the dinner table, slapping the children and their mother across the face and shoving them out of the room. He would stand over them screaming obscenities and telling them how worthless they were. He would break other pieces of furniture and their personal items.

Her home life was nothing that could be called ideal. It was joyless, anxiety ridden and filled with cover-ups for her father's behavior. Her mother would rationalize it, telling her how stressed he was and how lucky they were to have such a nice home, cars, etc. In his defense, she would say how fortunate they were—they would not be able to afford medical care, clothes, school supplies or any of the nice vacations that they took without him. After all, if he wasn't around to take care of them, they would be out on the street.

Her father's behavior and her mother's acceptance of it were constant throughout her childhood and adolescence. Annie could not bring friends home due to his behavior and she was rarely allowed to go to anyone's home. She felt lonely and was left out of peer's activities because invitations finally stopped since she never went.

Her fingernails were almost non-existent as she chewed them to the nub and her stomach was in constant upheaval. She couldn't concentrate very well at school and although she never failed a grade, she didn't excel at anything either.

Her brother began acting out and in his teen years that included run-ins with the police. This prompted more violence with her father and would result in huge fights between her brother and father that she was sure were going to result in death to one of them.

Annie wanted out—her inner desire was to leave home as soon as possible even though she worried about what would happen to her mother after she and her brother were gone. She thought if she could make enough money, her mother would leave and come live with her. Annie attended Cosmetology school, and landed a job right away. Within a few years, she was offered the opportunity to buy the business from the current owner. Being a successful business owner for 15 years hasn't erased her past.

She married at 23 to a seemingly nice man with a job in banking. Not having children was a choice Annie made early on. She felt she didn't have the skill base to parent a child and did not ever want to give up her independence like her mother had. If Annie was to describe their relationship, she would say that he was often mean "with his mouth" but not physically violent. Her husband would say very cruel and demeaning things to her in front of friends. He did not drink or use drugs. Blaming herself, she felt she must be setting him off somehow—she had probably never learned how to be a good wife due to her own upbringing.

Annie thought she needed help with relationship skills. It was obvious to me that Annie was living the same emotional life she had as a child. Her barometer for abuse was skewed as she measured it against direct violence. If it wasn't a physical type of assault, it wasn't violence, or so she thought. Something like the verbal abuse that someone else would never tolerate never registered with her as abuse as it was not as bad as the physical abuse she had once endured when under her parents' roof. Although she had financial freedom through her business, she did not use it to get away from the ongoing problem. Instead, she was looking inside herself for some inherent defect—it must be her fault.

I suggested that we start with some work designed to lessen her symptoms of anxiety. This would help her to focus. We also needed to spend time on the areas of attachment and boundaries. Although her mother had not directly abused her, allowing the father to do so damaged the mother-child relationship as well. Having Annie understand that these were issues she had learned, not something that was wrong with her was critical. My work with her would begin to build the skill base she needed to function as an adult with the wherewithal to take better care of and demand more for her emotional world. In working through the *Dysfunction Interrupted* program, she would also gain the advanced thinking skills and enrichment required to eliminate the ongoing depression and add some joy and hope to the expanded hole in her life.

This was a new world to Annie. She wanted help with her relationship skills and would be taught things that were foreign to her. Not much advanced thinking goes on in a household haunted by abuse. Lastly, but very importantly, would be the relationship work itself; she needed to be prepared to handle the potential outcome that I saw coming: the jerk of a husband might need to go.

What's Happening ...

Childhelp is an organization dedicated to the prevention of child abuse, and it compiles national child abuse statistics. The numbers are revealing.

According to *Childhelp.com*, it estimates that there are more than three million reports of child abuse and neglect made every year in the United States alone. These reports often include multiple children involved within one household. It is estimated that six million children were involved in 6.3 million child abuse reports in 2012. New reports are added every ten seconds.

These are just the ones reported. As a result of abuse, almost five children die every day in the US. This abuse occurs at every socioeconomic level, across ethnic and cultural lines, and within all religions and all levels of education. Further, it is reported that more than 60 percent of people found in drug rehabilitation programs were abused as children. In addition, 31 percent of women and 14 percent of men in prison report being abused as children. Some 30 percent of childhood abuse survivors will go on to abuse their own children. Eighty percent of young adults who were abused as children meet criteria for at least one psychological difficulty.[1]

Child abuse is a very difficult topic that brings very strong emotions to the surface. I'm not going to ask you

> If there are two parents and one is standing by and allowing the abuse, the allowing parent is also an abuser.

to think about being abused or to rehash every detail and incidence as I find that to be counterproductive. The goal isn't to cause you to experience more negative emotions. Instead, it is to instill hope and teach the ability to experience positive emotions.

The task at hand is to be able to see clearly how prior abuse is affecting you today. How could you develop proper and positive thought patterns as a child in an abusive environment? Sometimes a client will say, "My parents were only trying to teach me right from wrong or make me a

---

[1] Statistics in this paragraph are from the Childhelp website, www.childhelp.org/pages/statistics#gen-stats, accessed April 13, 2012)

better person." Whether there was actual abuse in the home or just discipline is unclear in her mind. My response is that if it felt wrong or excessive, it probably was.

Disciplining a child, even physically, shouldn't leave bruises or cause emotional scarring. I'm not talking about a whack on the behind or even a hand slap, but forceful violence. This violence is typically accompanied by an irrational rage. The child is terrified and wonders what they could have done to deserve such an attack. If there are two parents and one is standing by and allowing the abuse, the allowing parent is also an abuser. Few think that they are also culprits. They are neglectful of their child's well-being, which causes the child to experience a sense of abandonment by that allowing parent.

Living with this type of dynamic causes a very fundamental problem for the abused child; there is no safety in the home. There is the confusion the child feels of loyalty toward the abusing and allowing parents versus knowing that what they are doing is horribly wrong. There is a sense of unhappiness in the home, mixed with fear, and this is not how we are intended to live. Children from these homes often report stomachaches, headaches, nightmares or an inability to sleep and general nervousness. Symptoms that begin in childhood almost always carry over to some degree into adult life. These symptoms may morph over time and manifest themselves in different ways but they remain present. An example of this is the child who experiences many stomachaches and then as an adult suffers from stress headaches. The symptom is still a physical manifestation of stress; it just changed its look. Can you remember having physical ailments as a child that couldn't be explained by something obviously medical?

These children also often exhibit fingernail biting, nervous tics, acting out, aggressive behaviors and refusing to go to school. What child would really feel safe going to school when his father may kill his mother during the day? The children may become introverted as they expect any interaction with an adult to become negative and result in direct abuse.

School grades and performance may decline as the child's anxiety is so high it blocks the ability to take in and remember new information. If the house is chaotic at night, there may not be a quiet place to do homework. Education and learning may even be discouraged by parents who call it "stupid." There are other children, particularly those in severely abusive situations, who will begin to dissociate or go into their own world of fantasy where nothing can harm them. These are called dissociative disorders, and they are a very serious set of difficulties that require professional help.

So what does all that mean for you? The major adult potential personal difficulties for individuals of abusive families are listed here and defined in Part II. Unfortunately, bullying often leads to a combination of many of the following. You will notice that many of the symptoms of the conditions below also overlap.

1. Abusive relationships

2. Anger and acting out behaviors

3. Anxiety and Anxiety Spectrum Disorders

4. Attachment problems

5. Attention problems

6. Boundary problems

7. Caretaking and/or Codependency

8. Depression

9. Disorganized or chaotic lifestyle

10. Feelings of worthlessness

11. Hopelessness

12. Hypervigilance - "Boy Scout Brain"

13. Learned Helplessness

14. Personality Disorders

15. Poor coping strategies

16. Post-Traumatic Stress Disorder (PTSD)

17. Relationship problems

18. Self-Esteem issues

19. Trust issues

20. Underachievement

21. Vague physical symptoms

Family members in abusive households report feeling like they are always "walking on eggshells" and waiting for the next explosion from the abuser. You never know what is going to set abusers off because they will often choose just about anything based on their mood and how their day went. These families rarely engage in social relationships or activities. They don't want others to see this parental behavior, or the abuser doesn't allow social interaction as a means of controlling the family. As a result, the children not only suffer physical and emotional harm, but also are deprived of the social experiences and learning necessary for complete lives as adults. It's common for these children to feel guilty, that some-how they created the abusive incidents. They may believe that they are bad and deserve the ongoing abuse due to inherent worthlessness.

The result ... many become bullies themselves, as a means of releasing the pent-up anger and frustration that cannot be directed toward the parent.

Don't be disheartened as these are typical responses and can all be handled. And don't feel overwhelmed; remember that this is a learning process and you can learn anything. Piece-by-piece, I'll break these down and help you move beyond the problems they cause you in your current life. The treatments for each of these symptoms are largely the same, simply with a different focus.

2

Verbally Abusive Parents ...
Meet "The Name Callers"

*"The power of hope upon human exertion,
and happiness, is wonderful."*

—ABRAHAM LINCOLN

J eannette could not imagine what her daughter had said that had
created such a commotion at school—a commotion that would
recommend she needed parenting counseling and therapy for her
daughter. This didn't set well with her. She was a bright career
woman who thought all was well at home and that included her
son, daughter and husband.

A teacher had reported that her daughter Brianna had repeated
some very disturbing things that had been said to her by her
mother. Noticing that Jeannette's daughter looked as though she
had been crying, the teacher had asked her what was wrong, and
the dam broke with tears cascading from her blue eyes. Brianna
was hungry but had become so distraught at breakfast that she
couldn't eat because her mother was discussing with her father
the possibility of sending her to a "Fat Camp" away from home

for the entire summer. This final feeling of emotional abandonment had been too much for her to handle.

It turned out that on a regular basis Jeannette would chide Brianna
about being a bit overweight; telling her that she would not have
friends; that people didn't like overweight girls and that she surely
could forget ever having a boyfriend as she got older. She would
even say that her daughter was an embarrassment to the rest of the
family whom she considered attractive—after all, none of them
had a weight problem. Jeannette then taped signs to all the areas
Brianna utilized in the home that stated *Fatty's Bathroom, Fatty's
Extra Strength Chair, Fatty's Big Ass Laundry Basket, Fatty's King
Sized Bed* and so on. The refrigerator had a picture of Brianna on it
in her bathing suit with a sign that read, "Do you really need to be
in here?" Brianna was just 9-years-old.

When confronted with all of this, Jeannette readily admitted
that she had said and done all of this and more. For several years,
Brianna had been gaining too much weight. She stated that she was
very strict with self-discipline in the home and her daughter's eating
was unacceptable. She bristled at the idea that both the teacher and
I were now questioning how she raised her children.

When asked if she saw this as a form of abuse she said, "Certainly
not, I'm helping Brianna not to grow into an obese adult with health
problems as well as social problems. We love our children very
much and want the best for them."

Probing into Jeannette's own upbringing, it turns out she experienced
similar treatment. Her father scolded, nagged and berated her and
her siblings into good behavior and high achievement at the expense
of their self-esteem and self-acceptance. If one of them did not
perform adequately in his view, it was rehashed at the dinner table
with the whole family encouraged to say terrible things in order to

"motivate" the underachiever of the moment. They were taught not *to want to feel like a loser.*

Jeannette described her marriage as satisfactory, denied substance abuse of any kind and did not describe any symptoms of depression. She did describe symptoms of anxiety and admitted to engaging in road rage daily. She was very annoyed that the school was involved in their lives like this as she felt her daughter had now made them look like a *whole family of losers.* Her ability to empathize with her daughter was almost non-existent. Her own emotions had been so damaged and deadened by her own upbringing that she had completely lost touch with

The grandfather participated in the shaming of his granddaughter's weight.

them. She didn't dare think out of the box her father had created. Still alive and living in the area, he participated at times in the shaming of her daughter.

My work was layed out in front of me. Jeanette was my new client. However, her daughter and son would be the direct beneficiaries of the work that we did.

What's Happening ...

Verbal abuse is another direct form of emotional abuse. These are the parents who call their children stupid, worthless, ugly, fat, etc. The context doesn't matter, nor that they try to pawn it off as a learning experience; this is abuse. Another form of verbal abuse includes saying things like "I wish you were never born," "You're so fat ... you'll never find a husband" and "You were a huge mistake."

Verbally abusive parents are childlike and cruel, trying to vent their own frustrations by hurting the child. They may be angry people in general, always looking for someone to blame or attack to make themselves feel better. These parents often argue that they love their children very much and are just trying to help them. Does a parent really think that this is helpful? Would their friends, employer or employees be grateful for that

Verbally abusive parents are childlike and cruel.

sort of input? Believe me when I say that the children from these families don't find it very helpful; they often struggle with the hurt of these abuses for most of their adult life. In many cases, they come to believe the very things they are told, as after all "their parents must know."

The list of adult personal difficulties that can be created for these individuals is similar to that of the people who were physically abused.

1. Anger and acting out behaviors

2. Anxiety and Anxiety Spectrum Disorders

3. Attachment problems

4. Attention problems

5. Boundary problems

6. Caretaking and/or Codependency

7. Depression

8. Feelings of worthlessness

9. Hopelessness

10. Hypervigilance - "Boy Scout Brain"

11. Learned Helplessness

12. Personality Disorders

13. Poor coping strategies

14. Relationship problems & trust issues

15. Self-esteem issues

16. Underachievement

There are only so many things that can go wrong in a human being emotionally, and again the treatment is largely the same using cognitive behavioral approaches.

3

Sexually Abusive Parents ... Meet "The Sickos"

"Yesterday is not ours to recover, but
tomorrow is ours to win or to lose."
—LYNDON B. JOHNSON

Sexual abuse has many faces, that of pedophiles with children, older men with teenagers, parents with children they consider their property and unfortunately older children who have been abused themselves abusing younger children and siblings. Sometimes there has been a combination of several types and the individual finds themselves perpetual victims of these predators. That was the case with Kathryn.

For Kathryn, her first encounter of abuse was generated by her stepfather. He had entered the family's life when she was four and her parents divorced. She had visits with her biological father every other weekend, alternating holidays and summers. The stepfather worked evenings and was home alone with her in the mornings before school—the time when he would abuse her. He would also look for opportunities when her mother would go shopping or was out with friends. Four-year-old Kathryn was told not to tell anyone what was going on or she would never be able to see her real father again because the police would not allow her around any men.

Fortunately for Kathryn, her real father sensed something was wrong and asked her if she was alright. She began to cry out of fear of never being able to see him again. He persisted and was able to pry the story out of her. Her mother's response was immediate and appropriate—including the removal of the stepfather from the home. Simultaneously, she filed for divorce and charges were pressed with the authorities. The family went for counseling and Kathryn saw a therapist who specialized in child sexual abuse.

When Kathryn was seven, she was abused by a 10-year-old boy on the school playground. He would get her alone and fondle her and tell her not to tell or she would be in big trouble with her parents and they would probably send her away for being such a bad girl. This went on for about a year until the boy's father was transferred for work. Kathryn was relieved when he left and reported feeling better almost immediately once the threat of abuse was removed. She had never said anything to her parents but had become increasingly anxious and tried to find reasons not to go out for recess. She felt too ashamed to tell anyone. Needless to say, there was no intervention and no follow-up counseling.

> Sexual abuse has many faces, that of pedophiles with children, older men with teenagers, parents with children they consider their property.

In junior high school, Kathryn became bored easily with boys her age and started dating boys in high school. She preferred the company of boys to girlfriends. Through activities and parties, she met older boys and men—many who had already graduated, some in their upper 20's who hadn't moved away and still hung around the high school watching sports and partying with the younger students.

They were often the ones supplying the alcohol, marijuana and drugs for the parties.

Attractive, Kathryn was popular ... and she was just 14. One man named Ben introduced her to drugs that were quickly followed with a sexual relationship. He took her to a clinic to obtain birth control and forbid her to see boys her age or participate in any other school activities other than the sports that he attended with her. She felt smothered and depressed. The very few friends she had were cut off. She quit the drama club and language club. Like a puppeteer, Ben controlled her life.

Her parents didn't understand what was going on. When she was home, it became a battleground. The family began having arguments about what her goals were and what she was doing with her life. Kathryn didn't look or act like a typical 14-year-old. Her choice of clothing and the way she dressed was a continual source of conflict and upheaval at home. In actuality Ben was choosing her clothing that was so provocative. The school principal actually brought Kathryn into the office to let her know her clothing was inappropriate. She was warned that she would have to change her style or be removed from school.

Kathryn was pulled in both directions, the desire to be free of Ben but afraid of losing his "love" and attention. He had her convinced that she would not amount to anything without his direction and that she would be alone in the world without him. He told her she was very special and lucky to have him to "help" her. She had shared the stories of her prior abuse with him and he had made the comments that as "damaged goods," her choices in the world would be slim.

His "helping" her included videotaping sexual scenarios with himself in the tapes, with just Kathryn and then with Kathryn and his friends. Unbeknownst to her, he was selling these tapes, something she found out later. Kathryn reported that she knew this was all wrong but felt "way in over her head" and was at a loss as to what to do. If anyone knew what was going on she would be ostracized from her family. Her only girlfriend was one of Ben's friend's protégés, a girl like herself. Marijuana became an almost daily use and the "taping parties" usually involved other drug use as well.

This was her life for three years—from the eighth grade until she was 17 and a junior in high school. That year Ben lost interest in her and replaced her with another 14-year-old. Kathryn felt lost and betrayed. She didn't fit in with her classmates and was not getting along at all with her family. Quitting school and getting a job became her next step.

> **Almost all perpetrators know it is wrong or they would not ask children to hide it. They know it is not OK.**

Over the years, Kathryn knew that men were attracted to her because of her looks—there was no shortage of men willing to pay attention, buy drinks or provide marijuana in exchange for sexual encounters. Although it appeared her ticket to what she wanted, sadly her looks drew all the wrong sorts of people into her life.

She felt worse and worse about herself and felt lucky to have any friends, even undesirable ones. Her mistrust of people grew. She didn't expect very much from them or even herself. She surrounded herself with people who really didn't matter to her so she would not be disappointed when they ultimately let her down.

By the age of 40, she had had many low paying jobs and terrible relationships with two marriages ending with disastrous results and was now in another dead-end job. Her lifestyle had worn her down; she was depressed, uninterested in life and lonely. Kathryn felt there wasn't much hope or happiness for her future, both were

non-existent—the thought of suicide surfaced. We had a lot of
work to do, starting with the subjects of hope and enrichment.

What's Happening …

To victimize a child sexually is sick.

This may sound like a harsh statement or label, but it is what it is. To
victimize a child sexually is sick. It is also sick for the other parent or
significant other (if there is one) to allow it to happen once they become
aware of the issue. The perpetrator themselves may have been abused
as a child but that is no excuse to carry on the cycle. There comes a point
where everyone has been exposed to enough literature, television, etc.,
to know this behavior is wrong.

Almost all perpetrators know it is wrong or they would not ask the children
to hide it. They know it is not OK. Adult children from these situations
share many symptoms with those from other types of abusive homes.
One of the biggest struggles for individuals who have been sexually
abused is confusing their identity and self-worth in terms of sexuality.
Personal issues may include:

1. Abusive relationships

2. Anxiety

3. Attachment issues

4. Attention problems

5. Borderline Personality Disorder

6. Boundary problems

7. Caretaking

8. Chronic anger

9. Codependency

10. Controlling behaviors

11. Depression

12. Guilt

13. Hopelessness

14. Hypervigilance - "Boy Scout Brain"

15. Infidelity

16. Learned Helplessness

17. Low self-esteem/feelings of worthlessness

18. Panic Disorders

19. Post-Traumatic Stress Disorder (PTSD)

20. Poor coping strategies such as self-medicating with alcohol, drugs, etc.

21. Relationship problems

22. Trust issues

Sexually abusive individuals come from all walks of life and a variety of roles. Many are relatives; some are strangers. Kathryn's story is too common and seen in therapy way too often. Individuals who have been sexually abused come from every socioeconomic status and ethnic group. They are the victims of selfishness, pedophilia, sex-trafficking and greed. They are also the victims of those who need to control as well as the narcissistic men and women who have no regard for the feelings of others.

> **If there are two parents and one is standing by allowing the abuse, the allowing parent is also an abuser.**

4

Substance Abusing Parents ... Meet "The Out to Lunches"

"Your life is much more important than
you can imagine ... it is your first treasure."
—MAYA ANGELOU

Maryanne's most vivid childhood memory was that of the police raiding her home on Christmas Eve. This wasn't something she had dreamed up after watching a Chevy Chase *Christmas Vacation* movie but rather something that occurred due to her parents' chronic drug abuse, manufacturing and sales. For as long as Maryanne could remember, her parents had smoked marijuana daily and used cocaine at night. They threw big parties where everyone would use drugs of various kinds and all types of behavior would ensue. She and her sister were encouraged to stay in their rooms during these parties but it was much more fun to watch and no one checked to see if they were really where they were supposed to be.

Her sister was her closest friend. They did everything together: walked to school and back, played and watched TV in the evenings.

Other children were not allowed in their home due to the drug paraphernalia lying about, the marijuana plants growing in the backyard and the dubious visitors that came and went at all hours related to drug sales. Sometimes, she and her sister were invited to others' homes and went when they could. They joined in school clubs and activities and explained that their parents could not participate due to work demands.

Her father served close to 10 years in jail after that Christmas Eve. Any invitations to other children's homes stopped abruptly. Visiting him with her mother and sister became drudgery on Sunday afternoons. When he got out of jail, he went right back to his previous self-employment in the drug world. Really disappointed, she felt the family couldn't truly mean much to him if he was willing to risk being sent away again.

Growing up, Maryanne always felt loved by her parents but that there was never any time that they were available to her for talking or processing her day or her feelings. As an adult, she resents what she realizes were actually dangerous circumstances in the home—there was no supervision; strangers were in and out; and it was not uncommon to have one or both of her parents passed out on the sofas. What she saw as magical stories told to her as a child she now sees as the products of her parents' inebriation.

Maryanne's life is in chaos. She struggles on a day-to-day basis with achieving what she would like out of life. Maryanne knows she drinks too much at night to the degree that she feels poorly the next day and misses out on half the day's productivity. She is bored, depressed and drinks for something to do and as a means of socializing with friends. Her nail salon business is doing OK, but it's not at the level she would like it to be. Her home is a disorganized mess, almost bordering on hoarder status. She wastes a great deal of time trying to find daily items from keys to clothing and business related papers.

In her midst are three dogs that destroy things and add to the chaos along with a cat and a bird—all the animals are rescues.

Her relationships with men have been as chaotic as her upbringing was and her home life is. Substance abusers and other types of abusers have been the norm. "Bad boys" attract her. The big plus is that her self-esteem is somewhat in place and that moves her to get rid of these types as fast as they enter her life. Maryanne feels lost and isn't sure how to "find herself."

My work with Maryanne would be quite far reaching. Attention and boundaries would need to be addressed as would coping mechanisms, goal setting and getting herself together. Caretaking was lurking in there as was the reported "depression." In other words, Maryanne almost needed complete re-parenting.

What's Happening ...

This brand of parental dysfunction is characterized by the intoxicated, stoned or "zoned out on prescription meds" parent or parents. The drug of choice may be legal or illegal but it has basically the same effect on the family. It renders one or both parents "out to lunch," meaning not being mentally, emotionally and/or physically available.

A lack of safety in the home or a feeling of things being out of control and unpredictable envelop the environment. An added element

It can feel like there is a void where a parent should be.

of danger is thrown in when parents become abusive when using their preferred drug. For a child, it can feel like there is a void where a parent should be; everyone knows that someone is not fully present but is there only in body.

That lack of safety, being out of control or void can occur not by intentional neglect or behavior choice by the parent but simply as a result of a serious illness or injury that leaves a parent unavailable to the child.

The range of potential personal and relational difficulties for these individuals is again largely the same as with abusive families. It includes the following:

1. Abusive relationships

2. Anxiety and Anxiety Spectrum Disorders

3. Attachment issues

4. Attention problems

5. Boundary problems

6. Caretaking

7. Chronic anger and acting out behaviors

8. Codependency

9. Controlling behavior

10. Depression/chronic sadness

11. Disorganized or chaotic lifestyle

12. Guilt

13. Hypervigilance

14. Learned Helplessness

15. Low self-esteem

16. Perfectionistic tendencies

17. Post-Traumatic Stress Disorder (PTSD)

18. Poor coping strategies such as self-medicating with food, alcohol or drugs

19. Relationship problems

20. Trust issues

21. Underachievement

22. Vague physical symptoms

The task here is to retrace and figure out what was missed and what needs to be learned. It can be done.

5

Depressive Parents ...
Meet "The Sad Sorts"

*"Pessimists fear becoming the dupes of
hope. Optimists enjoy hope's company and
consider being duped no great matter."*

—MASON COOLEY

Debbie was tired—tired of a dead-end career that she dreaded
working in on a daily basis. She was exhausted with the care
of two children under the age of 10 and she got little support from
her husband in their care. Feeling overwhelmed at times, she felt
a genuine ongoing sadness and a lack of energy. Her husband had
a good job but spent his free time playing golf and hanging out
at their country club playing cards, leaving him little time to help
around the house or with the children. Her exhaustion and lack
of time meant that she didn't engage in hobbies or sports and
rarely had time to spend with her friends.

When Debbie thought about her upbringing, two things stood out:
her father was mostly absent due to work travel and her mother
slept a lot, taking long naps in the afternoon. She and her sister
were expected to play quietly so as not to bother her.

Debbie's mother didn't work outside the home. She rarely was up in the morning which meant Debbie and her sister pretty much got themselves ready and off to school. When she thinks of her mother, lethargic always comes to mind. Her mother was diagnosed with depression and was treated with a variety of medications throughout her childhood and teen years.

It wasn't always that way for her mother. She had studied advertising in college and aspired to work for a big firm in New York. She was offered a good position upon graduation and accepted. After marriage, Debbie's father received an offer from a law firm in the Midwest and insisted that they would be happier there due to a lower cost of living and better lifestyle on the money they would make. Debbie's mother acquiesced and the couple moved to Kansas. She never attempted employment again—the first baby arrived within the year after they moved.

From the time that Debbie can remember, her mother had been depressed, sleeping a lot, emotionally absent as she sought to lose herself in books and television and medications.

If there were ever problems at school or with classmates, Debbie's mother's attitude was, "Things just happen. There is not much you can do about it, so just study and get through it." Friends were not often welcomed into the home as it was a huge effort for her mother to make extra food. Besides, the noise bothered her. Debbie and her sister would sometimes sneak friends in and then play quietly in the basement or in the yard. Her mother was too tired to attend school plays or activities. There was never any conversation regarding future goals for the girls other than they would attend college and study something "reasonable," graduate and get jobs or marry.

Debbie was offered a job after graduating from college with a degree in marketing. Her parents told her she was lucky to be offered anything and she should accept even though it was in a city she didn't want to work in. Within a couple years of graduating, she married and started her family. Debbie continued to work although she was not crazy about her job—hopefully, it would be a stepping stone to something better.

She felt like she was in déjà vu—living her mother's life. Was she really her mother all over again?

Her children were strong-willed and highly energetic from the time they were toddlers. She was unsure how to handle them and tired by the end of the day. Most likely, some of their behavior was normal childhood behavior but seemed excessive given her own quiet walking-on-eggshells upbringing. She was considering taking them to a pediatric psychiatrist for ADHD medication to quiet them. Temperamentally, they appeared to be more like her husband. Debbie suspected that her husband's extended stays after his golf games were primarily to avoid the chaos at home.

Debbie's mindset was that she was lucky to have a job, husband and family and that she must be crazy not to feel happy. Surely, there must be something wrong with her. All of her negative feelings about things were then turned inwards on herself, draining her energy and causing her to feel increasingly hopeless. She believed that things just happened to her and that she didn't have much say in any matter. The result was that she was becoming more depressed as things got worse at home as well as in her job, a job she didn't like.

Was it hopeless? No.

Debbie saw it as a problem with depression on her part but I saw it with a different lens. She had problems with her self-esteem, locus of control and thinking skills. As I saw it, what Debbie needed to learn from me were problem solving skills and parenting information/

strategies. Both would allow her to feel in charge of her life and include realistic developmental expectations for her children that would place her in the driver's seat of her active children. She also needed to learn to move her *locus of control* (to be discussed later) from one of external to internal.

What's Happening ...

These homes are characterized by a sense of sadness and gloom. The environment tends to lack stimulation and fun, and it can feel cloaked in misery. If just one parent is depressive, the other may escape a lot and leave the child to cheer up the dysfunctional parent. Depression may be the main topic of the household, and the family members are all a captive audience of the depressed lifestyle. By this, I am not referring to an individual who experiences a sad episode or an episode of grief from loss or injury and works it through. Instead, I'm talking about the depressed person who remains stuck and doesn't seek treatment.

These parents are typically unavailable emotionally.

This type of depression may be the result of not fully understanding the condition. These individuals typically have learned poor thinking patterns from their own family of origin. They may believe they have a "disease" or a genetic or medical condition. There are also individuals who experience a "gain" from being depressed as they believe they won't be abandoned by their spouses while they are "sick." They may also receive inordinate amounts of attention from family, friends and doctors. Depression can remain, even with medications and treatments of all kinds, if the true cause of the depression is not uncovered.

The dynamic in the family may be characterized by an overwhelming sense of discouragement and hopelessness. The depressed individuals believe that it is impossible to experience happiness and will convey that belief to other family members. These parents are typically unavailable emotionally. The self-images of one or both parents are usually poor, and they see themselves as inadequate and unsuccessful with no hope for change. They may dwell on past events and overlook any positive features of life. They typically possess defeatist and fatalistic attitudes about all matters and in general "expect the worst." They are the eternal pessimists.

The messages to the children are typically that "you are not in control," "luck has passed us (and you) by" and that "no matter what we do things are not improving." For those affected by this dynamic, there is an entire research base pertaining to pessimism. There is also an extensive research base examining maternal depression and its effects on children's development.

Another common message pertaining to depression which is handed down to children: "We're all depressed in this family, it is genetic, and you come by it naturally enough. Go get some medication." This personality style or family dynamic often instills in the children poor coping strategies, hopelessness and victimization, with poor thinking similar to the thoughts of the depressed individual. The impact of all of this over the lifespan is huge in terms of quality of life. Well, you don't have to be depressed because your family members were. However, there are actually a few forms of depression that are genetic or that have biological underpinnings that will be identified in Part II.

A more serious element of this condition exists if suicide is discussed or threatened by the depressed parent. As harsh as it may seem, I believe that making children aware of these intentions or thoughts is also abuse. It then goes back to a lack of safety in the home. The children may be afraid to go to school for fear of the parent killing him/herself during the day. Whether the suicidal ideas are real or selfish manipulation, it holds everyone in the house an emotional hostage. Imagine children who are noisy in the morning, go to school, and come home to find that their parent has committed suicide. The children may incorrectly blame themselves forever for having caused this. As a parent, if you truly feel suicidal, it is your duty to get help, not make everyone in the family suffer with you.

Below are the potential personal difficulties experienced by adult children of depressed parents:

1. Attachment issues

2. Depression/anxiety cycle

3. Feelings of worthlessness

4. Financial problems

5. Hard to be around - no fun

6. Lack of joy/pessimistic view of life in general

7. Learned Helplessness

8. Locus of Control problems

9. May underachieve in academic as well as career settings

10. No goal setting - why bother?

11. Nothing to look forward to in life

12. Poor coping strategies

13. Relationship problems

14. Self-medicating

15. Trust issues

16. Underachievement

These scenarios are common. They can almost always be traced back to issues in upbringing, self-esteem and knowledge versus something medically wrong. The trick is to pull it apart and address each problem.

6

Histrionic Parents ...
Meet "The Theater People"

"If you are going through hell, keep going."
—WINSTON CHURCHILL

When Greg first met people, he typically held back, usually waiting for an invitation or a request to engage in conversation or enter a room. Most thought he was extremely shy and on the nervous side. What they didn't realize is that Greg had ongoing bouts of anxiety and panic attacks.

The death of his mother six months ago had landed him in his internist's office with mounting gastrointestinal problems, the inability to sleep much and increased panic attacks that were now surfacing at work. She had been a colorful and charismatic person in the community he grew up in. People had loved her.

Greg's emotions around the death of his mother were at direct opposites. His friends thought that his increased health problems were due to what he was feeling as a tragic loss and were seeded from the grief he felt. That wasn't the case. He was sad his mother had passed away, but he was also quite relieved and he felt extreme guilt because of it. The relief her passing brought to him transitioned to self-disgust—he must be a terrible son. And since he genuinely wasn't grieving himself, how could he console and support his father?

His family life was anything but typical and more like the *Addams Family* or horror fiction. Greg's mother was indeed colorful, but there was a darker side to her that had created chaos in the lives of those closest to her—the family. Her need for attention was bottomless and she would do anything to keep the family living in a type of three-ring circus. His mother was the ringmaster.

The annual celebration of Halloween is routinely looked forward to by kids of all ages. Not so for Greg—he would start dreading it as early as July. Terror would fill his young body as he knew what was coming. His family sponsored a hayride on their Midwestern farm, a hayride that was the talk of the region. Within the farm was an historic cemetery that included deceased family members.

During the month when most kids were planning costumes and looking forward to the Trick or Treat evening, Greg and his brothers were digging holes between the graves. Their "job" was to lie in the holes and be covered with dirt using scuba tubes to breathe and to pop up as the hayride went by and scare the bejeepers out of the participants. He was terrified as he lay in the ground next to the real graves; at the age this started he believed in ghosts himself and thought surely they were going to bring about something bad on all of them. He would start to hyperventilate in his hole and have to sit up between rides while his brothers calmed him. The entire month of October was spent buried in dirt.

When Halloween was over, his mother's attentions moved from the ground to the skies during the winter months. UFO sightings were her personal favorite and she felt that the winter sky was clearer and the best for viewing. This viewing was done from the children's bedroom located on the third floor of the farmhouse. She would invite friends over for the viewings and they would turn into big parties. At the age of nine, Greg believed in UFOs and spent his nights fearful that he would be abducted by an alien. The combination of nightmares and sleeplessness became his nightly companions— when he woke in the morning, he was tired and had a hard time concentrating in school.

When winter passed, spring was next and Greg's mother was ready. She created visions of "fairy elves" dancing in the children's heads— fairy elves that reportedly ran amok on their property causing mischief and mayhem. Greg never saw any of these but said his mother would warn them every day as they walked to the bus to beware not to anger the fairy elves or they would be sorry.

Greg's teachers finally requested that he be tested for ADHD. He certainly met the criteria as it is very similar to that of an Anxiety Disorder. He was given an entire battery of tests and commenced therapy. Greg liked his therapist and shared all the family events with her. His mother loved going to the clinic, talking to all the doctors and his therapist, it was another stage for her. She began paging the therapist during the evenings to tell her he was "up to something," or "not studying," or "being disrespectful." She would sometimes just make up issues or crises; call the clinic and demand that the whole family be seen at once.

If he was doing well, the therapist would recommend a break from therapy, a break that didn't fit into his mother's plans. She would then do something to set off his anxiety attacks so they could continue to go to the clinic at least weekly. Greg remembers his mother deciding to have a séance on a card table out in the cemetery, hiring a local psychic to run it during one of their school breaks.

The entire family was required to participate. For them, the séances were not new; his mother would usually run them and include her friends. What was new was having one in the cemetery. For his mother, she wondered why she hadn't thought of using the cemetery for the backdrop before.

The séances and the cemetery terrified Greg as much as the UFO viewings. And they affected his siblings who had their own reactions ranging from anxiety to depression to an eating disorder in one sister.

College broke him away from her overbearing influence, but she didn't disappear. Marriage and having his own children didn't filter her ability to create crises and "events" that included everyone. He couldn't move far enough away. Each phone call would suck everyone into her latest fad or dilemma. His father's protests throughout the years to any of this fell on her deaf ears. If any of them crossed her, she would throw everything off the table or break things that were lying around in fits of anger. Greg and his siblings learned that it was easier to just go along.

What's Happening ...

My professional side understood Greg's long history of anxiety problems. In fact, I questioned in my mind if he was ever really ADHD. In children these symptoms are very similar. I also understood the relief of having this person out of his life, a person who had tormented him to some degree his entire life. Although it was natural for Greg to feel guilt when he felt "relief" that she was finally gone.

Greg had been in therapy as a child and teen, having been referred by his teachers and pediatricians for psychological and educational evaluations as well as multiple rounds of therapy. He was thought to be suffering at that time from ADHD, was medicated and received special assistance throughout his academic years with testing and tutoring. All the symptoms that were troubling him before his mother's death were similar to what he was reporting now.

Family and Individual Dynamics

These parents or individuals within these families tend to be over-reactive, expressively dramatic, highly emotional and perhaps theatrical in their responsiveness to situations. There is the need to be the center of attention, and the parents may constantly seek reassurance from within the family as well as from outsiders. On an individual level, these parents appear to be vain and demanding. They will actively manipulate circumstances to keep attention on themselves. Their judgment is typically poor, thinking is scattered, and the family unit will most likely be chaotic and anxiety-provoking to members. Moods of the parent or parents are fickle and rapidly shifting, and they may be easily angered or bored. This family system feels very out of control to other family members.

Chaos runs rampant with constant distractions to any productive sort of activities.

The parents can be embarrassing at school or at home with peers, to the point that the child doesn't want to bring friends into the household. The parents' dress, mannerisms, or choice of peer groups may be embarrassing to the child. The child might be used for attention-getting, in matters of dress, artistic or musical accomplishment, etc., and he or she may be paraded around like a pet. When the company goes home, the child may no longer have the parents' attention—he or she becomes "out of sight, out of mind"—invisible until the next drama or event is displayed. There may be sexual acting out in the home, wild parties or huge domestic dilemmas involving the police.

Typical reactions of family members are to try to solve the crisis, to try to fight the system and become controlling themselves, or to dive right in and let it suck the life out of them. Chaos runs rampant with constant distractions to any productive sort of activities. There are usually no boundaries in place among family members, and there is a non-ending supply of crises that are usually at their finest around holidays and family events. These family systems are typically hard to break away from, as the parents will act out around you as you try to disengage.

Below are the potential personal difficulties experienced by adult children of histrionic parents:

1. Abusive relationships

2. Anxiety

3. Attachment issues

4. Attention problems

5. Become easily bored

6. Chaotic and disorganized with your own life

7. Codependency and Caretaking

8. Depression

9. Family estrangement

10. Guilty feelings of not doing enough

11. Intrusiveness of the family system can extend to your partner and children.

12. Learned Helplessness

13. Low self-esteem

14. Poor boundaries

15. Poor coping strategies

16. Relationship problems

17. Self-medicating

18. Trust issues

19. You do not learn emotional regulation and self-soothing.

For Greg, our treatment together would focus on several of these things, and allow him a view into his mother's mind in order to better understand the distress and suffering she inflicted upon the family. In understanding the developmental stages he was in when all this started, he could also begin to conquer the anxiety that had ruled much of his adult life as well. Included would be Biofeedback which would teach Greg how to overcome the nervous tics he had and calm his body.

7

Abandoning/Emotionally Unavailable Parents … Meet "The Here Today, Gone Tomorrows"

> *"Ah, hope! What would life be, stripped of thy encouraging smiles that teach us to look behind the dark clouds of today, for the golden beams that are to gild the morrow."*
> —SUSANNA MOODIE

Helen's behavior toward those she loved could be described as a scene out of Dr. Jekyll and Mr. Hyde. Her emotional challenges, reactions and changes had propelled her husband Ron to say, "I'm done."

When Ron traveled for work, Helen would call multiple times, usually in the evenings. If he didn't or couldn't answer, scathing messages were left about how she knew he was cheating—she was no fool and he would pay for his actions. Later, she would call back and apologize profusely and beg for forgiveness. The pattern would be repeated the next evening or when he went on his next business trip.

From her perspective, every slight mood change in Ron was a sign that the relationship was changing and that he was up to something. She constantly went through his things looking for evidence of affairs. After obtaining assurance that things were fine, she would become pleasant again, until the next episode. Helen was not a substance abuser, kept a good job and was good with finances. She had one or two good friends but rarely participated in social activities, preferring instead to spend her time with Ron. When he spent time with his male friends, she didn't like it and would call or email numerous times during any gatherings with them. Embarrassed, Ron stated that he became the brunt of his friends' jokes.

From the outside, Helen's upbringing and home life was a roller coaster of emotions starting as far back as she could remember. Her mother and father fought frequently and her mother would go into rages where she would scream at him, scream at Helen then disappear for a period of time—no one knew where she went. Minor things would set her mother off, even her father leaving clothes on the floor.

It was not so much the fighting between her parents that caused Helen the emotional distress she felt growing up. Rather it was when her mother would turn on her and declare that if Helen wasn't in the picture, she could leave forever, then adding maybe she would anyway and then she would disappear. As a child, Helen was terrified her mother would not return.

The really bad times were when she had done something to set her mother off. She would be told how bad she was; that she deserved to be given away to a detention home; and how she was really a problem for the family. Being gently corrected or taught what she had done wrong never occurred. Helen believed herself bad and unlovable and everyone would be better off if she ran away.

The isolation she felt was the source for distancing emotionally from her family, feeling that either she or they would inevitably be leaving anyway and there was no point being surprised and crushed when it happened. The distancing trickled into what friendships she had during adolescence and early adulthood. If there were small disagreements, she felt why bother to try and repair them—they would also leave her and be gone from her life.

As Helen began to date and enter relationships with men, she was very eager to please them for fear if she did not, they would leave. She also said that when she felt she was being "good" and they seemed distant or wanted to do things without her it was a sure sign that they were leaving. She said this made her feel "crazy." Not wanting to be hurt or abandoned, she would leave the relationship before the partner could leave and hurt her. On the surface, Helen knows that her behavior with Ron is unreasonable. Yet, she has no idea how to correct it as she feels she is in for more pain and rejection. She believes she will eventually just be alone.

Although Helen and her husband had been in marriage counseling, the counseling and coaching she needed far exceeded "could this marriage be saved." She would describe her husband as kind and good. Yet, their relationship was plagued by extreme jealousy and clinging by Helen combined with periods where she just disappeared for days on end. The modeling she had from her mother had been effective.

It was clear to me that one of Helen's major issues had to do with attachment. On top of that were difficulties with self-esteem, anxiety and sense of self. Self-soothing and biofeedback were on the top of the list of things to do to start to reduce Helen's fears and discomfort. Whether Ron was a good fit for her as a partner or if she had chosen him in desperation not to be alone was not apparent to me. That could all be figured out later on when Helen's primary issues were resolved. There was a lot of work to be done.

What's Happening ...

This dynamic can be carried out by either parent or both. It can take the form of actual physical abandonment or the emotional abandonment of a child. Threats of abandonment are also included, as children don't know if a parent says these things to motivate them to be good or if the parent really means it.

Adopted individuals often suffer some of these difficulties, as well as individuals from step-families or divorced families where one parent does not uphold responsibilities to the child after separating from the family. A death of a parent may also

Feelings of impending abandonment in these children are prevalent.

trigger these symptoms, as well as the loss of a parent who is hospitalized for long periods. When parents fight with each other and one then threatens to leave all the time, the feelings of impending abandonment in children are prevalent.

When actually abandoned, the idea or core belief is established in the child of being unlovable or unwanted. These parents are usually suffering from an attachment disorder themselves, starting in their own childhood. It was imprinted on them that if you don't please the parent, love may be withheld. A belief that is then passed to their children.

Statements heard in these households include:

I am going to call the orphanage and give you away if you don't behave.

I am going to call the snake farm and see if they're hungry today.

I don't care what you do; I give up on you.

You want me to stop this car and put you out?

You can all stay here by yourselves, I am leaving. Fend for yourself.

Sometimes these individuals actually do leave for undetermined periods of time, creating great stress and sadness in the children left behind. Sometimes they come back, and sometimes they don't.

Individuals growing up under these conditions do not handle separation well, as they expect to be abandoned. That pending abandonment feeling can be fueled by very subtle things, like a partner being distracted or non-attentive. When in relationships, there is a pervasive feeling and belief that the other person will eventually be gone.

Below are the potential personal difficulties experienced by adult children of abandoning/emotionally unavailable parents:

1. Abusive relationships

2. Anxiety Disorders or symptoms

3. Attachment Disorders

4. Borderline Personality Disorder

5. Caretaking and Codependency

6. Chaotic Lifestyle

7. Clingy/needy behavior

8. Compulsive behaviors may develop

9. Depression

10. Desperate relationships/relationships that happen too fast

11. Disturbances of mood, cannot self-regulate and experiences emotions in extremes

12. Extreme jealousy and possessiveness

13. Lack of confidence, self-esteem issues

14. May be poor at self-soothing

15. People-pleasing behaviors to detriment of self

16. Poor coping strategies

17. Relationship problems

18. Trust issues

The fear of abandonment can create paralysis in relationships. In Helen's situation, it threatened her marriage and her few friendships.

8

Invalidating Parents …
Meet "The Pooh Poohs"

"Your work is to discover your world and
then with all your heart give yourself to it."
— BUDDHA

Jenny grew up thinking she had an idyllic childhood. Her parents were the storybook of perfection—always there for her. Forewarning and preventing her from making errors, they were her guardian angels.

Her parents were kind and well-meaning. They simply wanted the best in life for their daughter. As many parents strive to do, they wanted to save her from making mistakes that could be avoided and bypass many of the bumps along the road of life. They believed if they taught her all the right things and corrected her when she was off track, she would have a smooth transition to adulthood.

In an ideal world that would work perfectly. However, with Jenny it did not work perfectly.

In their enthusiasm to save her from the typical and not-so-typical worries, inconvenience and problems in life, her parents began to do most of her thinking for her. They didn't listen or pay attention to her individual thought processes. After all, her parents knew best.

Growing up, her parents had "pooh-poohed" her questions and thoughts, telling her instead what the "correct" way of looking at things was. Jenny's view of the world was much different from her parents' "correct" thoughts; she began quite early to believe that most of her thoughts and the resulting feelings were off base and of little value.

Being a tomboy, she preferred outdoor sorts of clothing made for comfort and use rather than dressing for fashion. Her mother told her those clothes would not result in her getting a husband and that she would not be popular in school if she wore them.

Jenny relented and dressed instead like a fashionista. The clothes she wore were chosen by her mother. In her thirties, her mother was her personal shopper—if her mother wasn't available, she would allow a salesperson to make her selections.

She was allowed to ride horses and her sanctuary became the barn where she could wear comfortable clothing and interact with others with like interests. By this time, she had learned or had come to believe that her thoughts and ideas were very different from other people's. She quickly learned not to share them in conversation with others. Instead, she let them lead and she followed along.

Jenny became a good follower. She let anyone lead and she happily trailed along, or so she thought. Her peers viewed her as very agreeable. She believed that her parents had been correct in squelching her "odd" ideas as she was enjoying popularity with her peers as well as with other adults. It never occurred to her to rebel against her parents. She loved them and knew they only wanted what was best for her.

As an animal lover, she hated hunting and fishing and the killing of any living creature for any reason other than self-defense. Her father was a hunter and discussed his outings at the table during hunting seasons. She remembers cringing at the details of his exploits. When she would protest and say how she didn't like his killing animals, she was given a lecture on how silly her thoughts were—reinforcing his comments with, "The animal population needs culling," etc. Not stopping there, he defended himself. "My beliefs are those of almost everyone and if you voice your own in public, you will be seen as a troublemaker and *weirdo*."

Jenny got it—only troublemakers and weirdos had the kind of thoughts she had. She also got that her personal feelings were irrelevant.

In eighth grade, she wanted to take karate lessons with a girlfriend. Her parents told her, "Karate is not a sport for girls. It will make you appear 'tough' and therefore you will be unpopular."

Popularity was a big deal to Jenny's parents. Both came from conservative backgrounds and had active social lives in their church and local politics. Their attitude about gender roles was firmly cemented in those pillars. If any of her thoughts or questions appeared to be in contrast to their beliefs or something that would rock the boat, they were squelched immediately. They were not up for discussion and her points of view were not considered. Jenny's voice didn't count.

At times, she wondered to herself where all her ideas came from. In order not to make the wrong move, Jenny consulted with her parents or someone else whenever faced with a choice or decision, sure that her own oddness would force her to make the wrong one. To anyone on the outside, all seemed to be going smoothly in her life. Jenny felt blessed to be where she was and thankful that she had her parents' guidance and support.

The type of parenting that Jenny was reared under is similar in symptoms to those with perfectionistic parents. There is likely to be learned helplessness, difficulty with decision making and a skewed locus of control. Jenny's perfect life wasn't so perfect.

She had a hard time making decisions and was fearful of new situations. This fear, coupled with procrastination, had repeatedly surfaced. The latest situation involved her career. Jenny had been offered a new job in her company that required her to move to a new town and take on new responsibilities. That meant moving out of the home she had been in for more than thirty years; it meant cutting the physical umbilical cord.

Her company did not know that most nights Jenny came home and discussed her work issues with her parents who helped her decide how to proceed and what to do next. She feared that losing this nightly interaction would result in her making mistakes that would ultimately cost her her career.

What's Happening …

These individual parents or family systems tell you how you should feel on an ongoing basis. When you feel something different, they invalidate it or ignore it (basically the same result). This erodes confidence in children as they don't know then what is correct, to feel the way they actually do or the way they are being told to feel. Such a situation creates a constant conflict in children's minds. They then begin to look to others to make decisions for them, not trusting their own judgment.

> **Invalidating parents make it difficult for a child to develop a clear sense of self.**

Statements that you might hear in these families include:

Don't feel bad; you should be happy.

That doesn't hurt; you are a big boy.

Stop crying; you're so dramatic.

You aren't gay; it's a phase you are going through.

You can't do that right. Let me do it.

Even healthy parents may say things like this from time to time. However, it is more the constantly critical and controlling sort of parents that do the damage with these comments. I have found that it is always a hurdle for clients from these types of families to learn to trust themselves and plan and carry through their own lives and goals. These parents can also be the ones that take over and do a child's homework or finish chores started by the child. The "helicopter" parent has become common in the 21st century, hovering above and around the child.

It's not uncommon for a child's opinions and thoughts to be ridiculed or pushed aside as nonsense. These patterns make it difficult for an individual to develop a clear sense of self.

Below are the potential personal difficulties experienced by adult children of invalidating parents:

1. Abusive relationships

2. Anger

3. Anxiety Spectrum of Disorders

4. Become overly dependent on others

5. Conflicted thoughts

6. Depression

7. Difficulty asserting oneself and setting boundaries

8. Difficulty with decisions and major life choices

9. Low self-esteem

10. May not set boundaries

11. Poor coping strategies

12. Poor parenting skills themselves, due to a lack of confidence

13. Relationship problems

14. Underachievement

As human beings, we go through the major developmental stages from birth similarly. How we look at things and process information can be radically different. These processes mixed with our personalities and temperaments typically are what allow us to develop our own sense of self and how we want to interact in the world. Jenny was no different. Her parents' over-reaching influence had almost erased her sense and value of self.

9

Perfectionistic Parents ...
Meet "The Never Good Enoughs"

*"What lies behind us and what lies before
us are tiny matters compared to what lies
within us."*

—RALPH WALDO EMERSON

Teresa is depressed. She doesn't have a job and would like one. Experienced in the travel industry, she has been passed by for promotions and eventually let go from various positions she has held due to lack of productivity. Common complaints are that she doesn't apply herself and typically underachieves. When she walks into a room, she slouches and rarely shows any animation when she speaks.

Married with no children, she feels her husband is demanding, rarely appreciates what she does and usually criticizes what she does with negative asides. She has given up bothering to cook nice things as she gets the same response whether she makes a four course French dinner or a hamburger so why go to all the extra effort of the French dinner? Teresa will admit to allowing food to burn or seasoning it poorly on purpose since it will be met with the same negative response. Experiencing a bit of glee, she views it as a payback.

Not surprisingly, she grew up in a home just like the one she now lives in. Dear old dad was a critical and demanding father who never let up and was never happy with her achievements. At times she recalls feeling very proud of her school projects but an "A" grade wasn't good enough. It needed to be an "A+." Her room was never clean enough and the clothes she ironed never had the perfect pleat. She was repeatedly told that she was a slacker and would never amount to anything if she didn't try harder.

Teresa really felt that she was trying hard ... obviously, she must be a big loser.

Her mother's relationship with her father was of the same mold, but being a child, Teresa could not see that her mother was under the same scrutiny as she was. She remembers her mother retreating into a book or the television rather than engage in a conversation about their day—her mother knew she would only hear that the day was "never good enough." It was never filled with the degree of achievement and success at things that her father seemed to expect or experience himself.

Instead, at dinnertime he became the Drill Sargent. He would turn it into an inspection of what she and her mother weren't able to achieve in any given day. If they had spent all day decorating the house for Christmas so that it was beautiful when he arrived, he would instantly find fault somewhere. Instead of admiring their work, he would instead notice that there was a piece of dirt on the stairs or that a light bulb had burned out and wasn't replaced in the chandelier. Teresa remembers thinking *why bother?*

For Teresa, the drip factor came into play. Her attitude found its way into all aspects of her life. It dripped to her first job and then her second. She did what was necessary to get by but never fully engaged herself or her skill base. Why bother? Surely someone would find something wrong with what she had done.

When she first met her husband, she recognized his attitude and behavior. After all, she had lived with it for some twenty years growing up. His dynamic was so familiar to her that she felt comfortable. He was something she understood even though she didn't necessarily like what he did. And she knew she wouldn't thrive around him.

Teresa has become angrier and angrier. His treatment of her is no longer acceptable and her ability to tolerate him and his orders is vanishing. Teresa wants more from life and herself, even to start her own business as a travel agent. She has had enough.

What's Happening ...

Perfectionist parents (and spouses) are anxious and typically insecure. They may be overly involved in status and keeping up with the neighbors so as to not be judged negatively. They tend to be overly critical, judgmental, and possess excessive expectations. These expectations may be spoken about directly or simply understood through non-verbal displays, such as ignoring a child when performance isn't up to standards.

These parents tend to believe that the things they say are motivating to a child, never unmotivating. In actuality, their words, actions and expectations are destructive to the child's self-esteem. Often perfectionistic parents have been raised this way themselves. They strive to prove to the outside world that they have it all going on, when emotionally they tend to be bankrupt. Money, success and status may be the manifestation of this need or great displays of talent or athleticism carried out by the child. The child's good grades and academic or scientific achievement may also be the outlet.

This is not to say that everyone whose parents pushed them to be successful was raised in a dysfunctional environment; there are many positive ways to achieve as well. Think about negative parents, the ones who made their children feel like they were never enough, their performance was never enough, and there was never enough success. These parents may be workaholics themselves or it may be one parent who is frustrated with their station in life and is living vicariously through the child. They may also withhold love based on performance.

Comments typical in these homes include:

That "A" is good, but why wasn't it an "A+"?

I'm glad you scored a touchdown. Too bad it wasn't the winning one.

Your brother got an "A+".

It was nice that you are in the school play but why didn't you get picked for the lead?

Below are the potential personal difficulties experienced by adult children of perfectionistic parents:

1. Abusive relationships

2. Anxiety and Anxiety Spectrum Disorders

3. Become controlling yourself

4. Become workaholic yourself

5. Codependency/Caretaking behaviors

6. Depression/anxiety cycle

7. Lack of joy/pessimistic view of life in general

8. Learned Helplessness

9. Locus of Control problems

10. May carry on cycle and become perfectionistic to a negative level yourself

11. May not set boundaries

12. May underachieve in academic as well as career settings

13. No goal setting - why bother?

14. Poor coping strategies

15. Poor parenting skills themselves, due to a lack of confidence

16. Relationship problems

17. Trust issues

Sometimes outright rebellion occurs. It is often prefaced with a passive aggressive response in a person who feels belittled and helpless. Teresa had lived with it for decades. She didn't want to slouch around anymore or play the silent stealth games to get back at her husband and in reality, her upbringing as well. She wanted to shake the past and the belittling she had endured.

10

Controlling Parents …
Meet "The Control Freaks"

> *"What lies behind us and what lies before us are tiny matters compared to what lies within us."*
>
> —RALPH WALDO EMERSON

Young, Tony is "rough around the edges." He's had run-ins with the law with the latest being a domestic dispute that resulted in his arrest. Tony has a history of minor assault that has come from bar fights. For him, anger is continually on the surface. His targets for venting it are usually walls and furniture.

On the outside looking in, he has a steady job and is an attentive father and husband for the most part. Inside looking out, he has a quick temper and is easily riled. The court has ordered that he get help with his anger management and learn skills to control it.

When it came to calming himself down after an outburst, he was typical of many men—he headed for a beer. If the beer didn't produce a calming effect, he started hitting walls or turning over furniture and yelling. The latest episode was the first time there had been any physical violence between he and his wife and she had called the police. Tony was remorseful and very frightened that he could have seriously hurt her.

It didn't take much to make Tony angry. In his view of conflict, he felt he needed to "do battle" to win—at times, it overwhelmed him. He lacked basic negotiation skills and felt that when there was any opposition to him, the other person's intent was to *do him in*. If the conflict was with a higher up in his company, he would remain quiet and drink it away later.

Tony's anger management therapist and I went spelunking into his childhood to find out who and what his models were. How was anger handled in the home? How did he respond to it? What did he do to calm himself down when he was enraged? His father was a hard worker in a factory and was a good dad, but spent a lot of time at his "lodge" playing cards and visiting with friends. He said that his parents seemed to have a good relationship and there was no outward fighting.

Tony's mother had suffered from anxiety attacks since her own childhood. She had been on valium and other anti-anxiety medications her entire adult life. She slept a lot, worried excessively about everything and avoided being out in public. His friends were rarely allowed in the house after school or on weekends. The noise and mess that they created was too much for her. Tony was not allowed to join any sports activities or clubs where injury was seen as inevitable. His mother needed control of her environment at all times. Under her influence, little problems became gigantic by the time they passed through her mental filter. What little energy she had was directed toward keeping an immaculate home.

His mother's method of coping was to retreat into valium as she didn't know another way to deal with her fears. She also gained comfort in controlling her immediate environment—things like Tony's life that were possible to control. She could not teach him how to deal with his fears as she didn't know how to deal with her own. Her intent was not to be a neglectful parent—she just didn't know how to be one. In fact, she probably thought she was helping him.

Tony never threw temper tantrums at home as he felt quite comfortable there. If there

Beer became his valium.

were conflicts or problems in school, he would go in the woods and kick trees and branches. Neither of his parents realized he lacked coping skills for facing the world.

Inside, he was afraid of most new situations and people. He had learned to look at the world through a mental filter of suspicion and caution. When he felt out of control of a situation it sent him into a whirlwind of anger and fear that he acted out in the physical destruction of things.

Beer became his valium. He expected every conflict to result in a major upheaval of his life. Disagreement with a coworker would mean he got fired. If his wife was unhappy with something, it would mean a divorce. Taking time to think through the issues wasn't an option, as no matter how much time he spent thinking about it, these were his preconceived conclusions. There was nothing wrong with Tony's brain; he just needed new thoughts, new skills and new calming procedures.

Tony believed that the world was a scary place with danger lurking everywhere—most people were out to get you in some way and they were not to be trusted. The message of caution was clear to Tony, but it was not very clear as to how one might go about dealing with this scary world.

He got that he just didn't get how to deal with anything that was a problem. His mode was to "fight or take flight"—both got him into trouble.

Fighting or exiting a sticky situation is a natural human occurrence when anyone feels threatened. The choice is usually based on the situation, a person's temperament, and thinking through the outcome. At a very base level, the reaction of fear or anger is not uncommon.

What's Happening ...

Controlling parents are typically suffering from anxiety and fear, chronic anger, or a combination of both. There are also the few who are chronic sadists, as in the other forms of direct abusers. This form of parenting often goes hand-in-hand with one of the other types of more direct abuse.

The other end of the spectrum are the types that suffer from a great deal of fear and are overprotective. They hope to spare themselves and their children any suffering or pain that can be prevented. These individuals have often suffered great losses themselves in life, such as the loss of a parent or another child, living through a war or other disaster, or a life-threatening illness or accident. Sadly, in their attempt to protect, they often rob the child of early experiences or any experiences that may be fun as they are deemed "too dangerous." If you came from this type of home, you know the feeling. There is the pervasive notion of fear and danger present in every move.

> **Controlling parents also may dictate clothing choices, career and college choice, friends and anything else to an extreme.**

Controlling parents also may dictate clothing choices, career and college choice, friends and anything else to an extreme. Please do not mistake this for the parents who do teach appropriate behaviors and set rules and standards. There is a difference. Controlling parents tend to smother and put out any creative life or spontaneous joy in their children.

There may have been extreme anger and control in dealing with you as a child and your normal child behavior.

Below are the potential personal difficulties experienced by adult children of controlling parents:

1. Abusive relationships

2. Conflicted thoughts

3. Dependent relationships

4. Anxiety Spectrum of Disorders

5. Become dependent on others

6. Chronic anger

7. Depression

8. Difficulty asserting oneself and setting boundaries

9. Difficulty with decisions and major life choices

10. Low self-esteem

11. May not set boundaries

12. No sense of self

13. Poor coping strategies

14. Poor parenting skills themselves, due to a lack of confidence

15. Relationship problems and trust issues

If You Had Controlling Parents by Dan Neuharth, PhD, provides great in-depth coverage of this topic and is recommended. If you have identified this pattern as that of your family of origin, I strongly encourage you to read his book as a part of completing this program.

11

Parents Who Do Not Discipline …
Meet "The Free-for-Alls"

"Life is like the ocean currents; if you know
not how to navigate, you're as good as lost."
—Greg Evans

A t 35, Len can't keep a job for long. When asked what he viewed the problem was, he would reply, "I don't know, I get the job done."

When pressed for details, he conceded he was often late to work and assignments were not completed on time, even admitting to spending considerable time on his computer games. Len never viewed being late as a *big deal* either, after all, he finally *came through* for the employer by completing his tasks. Past employers had repeatedly documented incidents and spoken to him or written up his lateness and non-completion of work. Len said that one human resource manager had told him he seemed to have a bad attitude toward his work.

Len's inability to discipline himself or accept direction from others has now affected his own marriage and parenting. He avoids discipline with his children and sees their misbehavior as "not a big deal." Losing his latest job, his wife said, "Enough," and insisted he get counseling. She feels alone in the relationship and is considering divorce if things do not improve.

His parents divorced when he was eight. There was nothing amicable about it—Len became the pawn used to attack and hurt the other during the legal proceedings and beyond.

"I give up. Do what you want."

If Len was allowed to eat on the sofa in his father's house, his mother made sure he ate only at the table in hers. The pattern that developed was one of the father's house being much more fun than the mother's. Dad's rules, or lack of them, were the favored set in his 8-year-old mind. He would behave by this set of rules in his mother's house with the result being an angry mother who would routinely say things like, "I give up. Do what you want." When she had the energy, she would attempt to discipline Len and if he resisted, back down immediately. It became the normal behavior between the two houses. As most kids do, Len figured it out and knew how to play each off the other.

Most parents work—Len's were no exception. Not surprisingly, they were tired at the end of the day. His father always called Len his "little buddy" and would bring home takeout food for dinner. Watching TV together most evenings, it was common for his father to fall asleep. The house then became a free for all for Len to do as he pleased with his friends. He would invite them over and head to the bonus room to make noise, jump on furniture, you name it. His friends—and he—thought it was a child's heaven of fun. If his father awoke from the noise, he would make a half-hearted attempt at stopping the ruckus by yelling at them and making idle threats of sending everyone home. Then he would just return downstairs to his TV and continue to nap.

In high school, Len avoided all sports and anything to do with teams—he didn't want the "commitment" of a practice every night. When it came to class attendance, he would often arrive late without his homework and receive detentions. For Len, he saw it as "not a big deal"—he felt the teachers were just exercising their power over him. Given that belief, he was never apologetic for his behavior, not very popular with his teachers, and viewed as the underachiever/slacker in the class.

At home he was given even more freedom as a teen and he would spend his time hanging out with friends or watching TV. He was not given chores—his parents had given up long ago, their attitude was that it was easier to hire someone to do things like mow the lawn than fight with him.

As Len shared his story, it became clear that his repeated terminations were seeded back to the patterns established as an eight-year-old boy. No rules, no commitments and no consequences. His well-established eight-year-old patterns were ingrained.

Len's background is what the psychology world calls "laissez faire" parenting. I call it "The Free-for-Alls" ... *free from all parenting* does far more harm than good.

What's Happening ...

These family systems may be characterized by chaos and anxiety, as there are no clear rules to live by. Sometimes the children are comfortable at home. However, they find themselves not popular or shunned with peers, as they don't behave by the same standards or manners. These children also may have difficulties with other authority figures or find themselves actually disliked by adults and their friends' parents. They may develop a sense of entitlement that hinders them in social, work and academic environments, as others do not bend to their wishes.

Parents who do not discipline often feel that they will lose the love of the child if they set and abide by rules, and they try to be the child's friend. Parents especially feel this way if they work all day or see the child for limited visitation, as in divorce. Such parents may not want to spend all contact with the child engaged in correcting behavior. A "free-for-all" parent may have been over-parented themselves, causing them to rebel too far and feel that setting rules and teaching appropriate manners is harsh or mean.

There is often a backlash to the lack of discipline, as behaviors that seem OK one day get on the parent's nerves on another. The parent then blows up, causing confusion and anxiety in the child.

These children may be indulged in every whim and are not taught any self-regulation skills. The children may expect teachers and coaches to bend the rules for them and be very upset when it doesn't happen.

Below are the potential personal difficulties experienced by adult children of parents who do not discipline:

1. Anxiety

2. Attention problems

3. Boundary problems

4. Career problems

5. Chronic anger

6. Depression

7. Disorganized lifestyle

8. Peer rejection

9. Poor coping strategies

10. Poor parent skills

11. Relationship problems

12. Sense of entitlement

13. Underachievement

Children don't need their parents to be friends—their friends come from their peers and classmates.

Get Ready to Interrupt Your Dysfunction

Summing Up

Have you noticed one or more patterns that you feel are applicable to your childhood? Most likely you were also able to initially identify with some of the listed difficulties.

In Part II, seventeen difficulties will be probed into in more detail to give you the full definitions. This will allow you to determine if they are the cause and roots of the challenges you face today.

You may have noticed many repetitions of the symptom sets across parenting styles. This is largely because there is only so much that can go wrong. Why you experience these symptoms differently than others is due to inherited traits such as temperament, your immediate environment and the way the different combinations of the symptom sets interact with each other. These many possible combinations may make your anxiety look very different than someone you know who experiences anxiety, but it is essentially the same.

Before moving to the next part, complete the five tasks on the following page. I know it may feel like a burden to be asked to do something like this. But I promise, I've made them simple and you won't have to spend a great deal of time on them.

What I do know is that they are necessary and will be helpful to you in planning and building a new life of your own design. Having a plan or "menu" simplifies things in the long run. It keeps you from getting sidetracked or overwhelmed. Keep a notebook or journal just dedicated to this program and your transformation for yourself for quick and easy reference.

Tasks for Part I

1. Identify which type or types of family pattern(s) you grew up with.

2. What types of family patterns did your parents grow up with?

3. List the symptoms that you believe you currently suffer from and those that you may have experienced in the past. These are defined in Part II. If you are not sure, just wait and list them after reading Part II.

4. If you are aware, list any emotional difficulties that your parents have experienced.
   Mother:
   Father:

5. Do you see repetitive patterns in family members ...
   Sisters, Brothers, Aunts, Uncles, Grandparents?

PART two

Defining the Problem

To create more positive results in your life, replace 'if only' with 'next time.' —Unknown

In Part I, the different family systems were identified that you might have grown up within. You may have also been able to identify ones that you believe your parents themselves experienced. A true story, with changed names, was shared before each description of a family style that was followed with a list of symptoms or "emotional ills" from which you may suffer currently or have suffered in the past. They may be ones that you always knew were present but didn't have a name for or ones that have been formally diagnosed for you by a physician or psychologist. They could have manifested themselves vaguely as a "feeling" that something wasn't right but you didn't know quite what it was.

Part II focuses on understanding these problems, being able to put a name to them, and therefore moving yourself further down the road to feeling and getting better. Once you have identified a problem, it is much easier to fix. Some of them, such as anxiety and depression, are very common terms with which you are probably already familiar. Other terms, such as Hypervigilance and Codependency, may be new to you. Throughout Part II, I have attempted to give you an overall definition and explanation to make the learning process as easy as possible.

In This Section

13

Anxiety and the Anxiety Spectrum of Disorders

One of the more debilitating problems we can experience is anxiety. It affects you psychologically as well as physically. It can feel like anything from a little nervousness to full blown panic and every sensation in between. You may know exactly what sets it off or it may feel as if it comes out of the blue. It may be specific in nature or it may be that you just spend the majority of your time and emotional energies worrying about everything. Your friends and family may call you the "worry wart."

With it comes physical symptoms such as sweating, rapid heartbeat, dry mouth, hot flashes, numbness and shaking. You may feel like you are going to faint or you're losing your mind. It may be hard to breathe and you feel like you

> It can feel like anything from a little nervousness to full blown panic and every sensation in between.

are having a heart attack or even dying. Gastrointestinal upset may follow. Very unpleasant business, all of it. The real kicker is you do not even have to be present with a specific stressor; usually just thinking about it can bring about the same results.

Anxiety is also the most common psychological problem with many parts to it. You certainly have experienced some anxiety so you know how it feels, but what you might not know is how it affects you on a daily basis.

Some anxiety and trauma related issues are given specific names or labeled as specific disorders as defined by *The Diagnostic and Statistical Manual of Mental Disorders* (DSM-5). This manual is designed and used by professionals for diagnostic purposes. These specific disorders include: Panic Disorder, Agoraphobia, Social Phobia, Generalized Anxiety Disorder, Post-Traumatic Stress Disorder, Acute Stress Disorder, Obsessive Compulsive Disorder, Agoraphobia without History of Panic Disorder, Anxiety Disorder Due to a General Medical Condition, and Substance Induced Anxiety Disorder.

Panic Disorder is the sudden onset of a set of symptoms or a fear response, sometimes seemingly out of nowhere. It can last several minutes and the individual often feels as though he/she is having a heart attack or going crazy and might faint. There may be gastrointestinal upset or nausea, temperature flashes from hot to cold, chest pain, shaking and a shortness of breath. Although it feels like it, these will not kill you. The secondary problem that then begins is the fear of having a panic attack in public or another one in general that keeps the individual in a state of alarm called **anticipatory anxiety.**

Social Phobia (Social Anxiety Disorder) involves fearing that you will embarrass yourself publicly. The fear is much greater than normal feelings of not liking to perform or conduct public speaking. Typically these individuals will avoid social functions, although some will medicate themselves or just struggle through out of necessity. The fears may be specific social situations such as choking or spilling food in a restaurant or may be general and include any situation where they may be watched or their performance evaluated by others. As with any of the conditions discussed here, Social Phobia only becomes a formal diagnosis if it meets the criteria under DSM-5 and takes away from an individual's ability to function properly across settings.

Generalized Anxiety Disorder is experienced as chronic anxiety that remains with a person across settings and has been present for quite some time. These are the true "worry warts" who spend considerable time worrying about many things and limit themselves in life experience by doing so. The anxiety can be very debilitating on a daily basis. Symptoms include irritability, restlessness, fatigue, difficulty concentrating and difficulty sleeping. Generalized anxiety disorder is often misdiagnosed as **Attention Deficit Disorder** as they share many symptoms. Generalized Anxiety Disorder can begin in childhood and may wax and wane during different stages of life.

Post-Traumatic Stress Disorder (PTSD) involves the development of chronic psychological symptoms after a traumatic event, either to you or a loved one. The event is one that carries with it the possibility of serious injury or death. The symptoms include flashbacks of the event, horror, panic, nightmares, anger, emotional detachment and repetitive thoughts about the event. Individuals may also attempt to avoid any situation similar or any cues reminiscent of the event. The symptoms last for prolonged periods and cause significant distress as well as limiting the individual in performance. Soldiers returning from war often experience PTSD as well as children from physically or sexually abusive environments. Survivors of plane crashes, train wrecks and car accidents or any episode of violence are susceptible as well.

Acute Stress Disorder is similar to Post-Traumatic Stress Disorder in its symptoms, however the emphasis on this disorder is that it subsides in roughly a month's time rather than becoming chronic. The trauma involves exposure or participation in an event that also carried the threat of serious injury or death.

Obsessive Compulsive Disorder (OCD) is characterized by repetitive thoughts or ideas or impulses that are intrusive and very hard to dispel. The compulsion part is the behavior that an individual performs to try and reduce the discomfort brought about by the obsessions. If you believe you have left the garage door unlocked you may want to check it. Persons suffering from OCD will check it 30 times as the idea that it is unlocked is still in their mind, even though they have seen for themselves that they did indeed lock it. It is a fascinating disorder but can be hugely debilitating as these individuals spend hours checking doors, light switches, stoves, etc. Germs and becoming contaminated is a common theme as is the belief that they may have hit someone with the car and need to go back to check or look for the body.

There may be a fixation with certain numbers to the extent the individual has to perform certain activities that number of times. For example, a person fixated on the number 30 may have to circle a parking lot 30 times before actually choosing a spot, or flick the light switch 30 times. Typically if the routine is interrupted, the person will need to start over.

There are different theories in the literature about the etiology of OCD. There are genetic theories, theories of head and brain injury, chemical imbalance and those of stress response. It can be seen in childhood but in others it may not make an appearance till their twenties or thirties. Some have one episode of OCD and others have a chronic battle for years.

Phobias are the extreme end of the spectrum and the individual suffering from a phobia will typically go to any length to avoid the feared object. Usually the fear is somewhat irrational in response to the actual threat presented by the object. The most common phobias are claustrophobia (fear of small spaces) and agoraphobia (fear of open spaces). What agoraphobic individuals may be most afraid of is having a panic attack or losing control in a public place, having no help or making a fool of themselves while this is happening. They then avoid this possibility by staying home. The process is quite complex and there are very interesting studies on the cognitive process that actually takes place in the brain in an individual suffering from a phobia.

There is a long list of phobias, everything from snakes to elevators to lightning. It is suggested that they develop from a personal experience in childhood or from modeling by watching a person such as a parent with a phobia. Research also suggests that the actual fear is not the item itself but rather the outcome of interacting with the item. These fears do not always result in severe disability of the individual, but on the other end of the spectrum are people who will not leave their houses or who go to great lengths to avoid the feared item.

Where Is the Anxiety Coming From?

First, **any related or causative medical disorders or illnesses** should be ruled out. The most common diseases that can underlie or cause the symptoms of anxiety include Hyperthyroidism, Hypoglycemia, Mitral Valve Prolapse, Hypertension, Cushing's Syndrome, certain mineral and vitamin deficiencies and Post Concussion Syndrome. Your physician can easily test for these to rule them out as causative factors in your anxiety problems. Another physical reason you may experience anxiety is that you have ingested too much caffeine. Coffee, tea, lattes, soda, chocolate, diet aids and energy drinks almost all contain caffeine. If you have overdone alcohol, there is an odd reaction in the brain that makes you experience higher anxiety the next day. People with alcohol problems may start drinking again to do away with the anxiety, therefore creating a vicious cycle. Medical theories suggest it is related to blood sugar levels. Obviously if you ingest cocaine, amphetamines or other stimulants, they will increase your anxiety as will some over the counter and prescription cold and allergy medications.

Examining the side effect sheet from any prescription medications you take can also be helpful in identifying a physical reason. Also ask your doctor or pharmacist if you are not sure.

With the medical ruled out, looking at **environmental stressors** is next, either present or over time. You have a biologically built-in protection system called "fight or flight." When your brain registers danger, it decides how to proceed and gives the body the automatic signal to react. This is normal and means your system is working beautifully, but you may be overworking it. In your life right now you may not have the physical danger you once were threatened by, but your brain picks up emotional or psychological trauma and reacts the same way.

> **You have a biologically built-in protection system called "fight or flight."**

Abusive relationships, chronic stress, arguments, etc., can bring about the same response.

When you grow up in a **highly dysfunctional home,** there is always the fear of the next tirade, the next insult, and the wondering of how your behavior will set off your parent. In the controlling or overprotective home, you are taught that every time you step out the door it may be your last due to all the inherent dangers in the world. Every cough may be pneumonia, every speeding car is careening to hit you resulting in paralysis and every van that drives by is a pervert looking to harm the innocent. It's not the normal things you are taught as a child about being careful, but the overdone variety where there is certain danger everywhere and in every circumstance. In a perfectionistic home, you may not be performing up to expected standards. In a home filled with substance abuse, there is always unpredictability. In the histrionic household, there is sure to be a drama unfolding that you will be part of. In a home where abandonment is an issue, the anxiety comes from wondering if the parent will actually leave or if the parent does leave will he/she come back. Who will take care of you if your parent leaves? The "pooh pooh" family creates its own brand of anxiety by instilling constant doubt about everything you are thinking.

What happens in these dysfunctional homes is that your brain becomes used to thinking in a certain way. Then off it goes, until these fears take on a life of their own in the form of panic attacks, phobias, physical ailments, tics, compulsions and social problems. Even long after you leave your parents' house, the thoughts remain as this has been your training ground. This program will help you to leave these thoughts behind and design beliefs of your own choosing. It will feel great!

Other Considerations

Everyone experiences fear to some degree. Not necessarily fear that your life is at stake but **ongoing fears,** such as fear of rejection, fear of illness, fear of not having enough or poverty. Fear is an important enough factor that a chapter on eliminating it or controlling it is in Part III of this book. When you fear these things constantly, it puts your body in a constant state of anxiety or arousal. It is this hyperarousal that causes your problems. This hyperarousal can actually alter your brain chemicals by oversupplying cortisol and adrenaline and the other stress chemicals that then take over the "brain space," not leaving enough room for the "good chemicals" that calm you. When you hear talk about chemical imbalances, this is usually what has happened as opposed to being born that way.

You are born with certain **temperamental tendencies** that may look genetic in that you see it in family members. Those temperamental tendencies, such as sensitivity, added to an environment of fear, chaos, trauma or disturbing emotionality then may dictate how you react or what coping skills you employ. However, this does not mean you are born disordered and cannot be well or relieved of chronic debilitating anxiety. It looks genetic but family members are just behaving the same as they all think the same. If your mother and her sister were raised in an abusive environment, they may both be anxious, depressed or suffering from Post-Traumatic Stress Disorder. Does this mean it is genetic? No, it means they both experienced something similar in childhood that brought about a significant stress response. If your grandfather, father and you are all depressed, it does not mean it is genetic either. Grandpa may have passed down a terribly negative thinking pattern that would suck the life out of everyone, including the family pet.

Anxiety takes a toll on the body. Being constantly on guard tires the system. Chronic anxiety has been related to high blood pressure, muscle spasms and pain, headaches, immune system weakening, gastrointestinal disorders such as irritable bowel syndrome, ulcers of the stomach, skin rashes, etc. Anxiety has a healthy place in your life in order to protect you, but a little goes a long way. You are best served to get it under control and use it only to your advantage, rather than let it run rampant. Anxiety is a natural event, but it needs to be roped in and the brain allowed to use it as it was designed.

14

Attachment Problems

A ttachment is defined as a special emotional relationship that invokes an exchange of comfort, care and pleasure. The late John Bowlby is considered a pioneer in the field and is given credit for Attachment Theory as it is now used. He describes attachment as the "enduring psychological connectedness between human beings." These early experiences have important influence on the development of relationships and our relationship behavior in later life. Attachment styles are developed in childhood through the child/caregiver relationship and also through early experiences with others.

Researchers believe there may even be an evolutionary aspect to attachment behavior as having a group around you to support and protect you certainly would ensure survival over the individual who was alone to fend for himself. Bowlby also believed that you have attachment needs across your entire lifespan, not just as a child, and this is where your romantic relationships come in as well as your behavior in friendships and with family.

> The adult behavior of securely attached children includes the tendency to develop trusting, long term relationships.

The 4 Main Attachment Styles according to the literature and research:

1. Secure Attachment: These children do not experience significant distress when separated from parent/s and when frightened will seek comfort from them. Contact with the parent is seen as positive and readily accepted by securely attached children. These children are not overly distressed by a parent's brief absence, but clearly prefer their parent/s to strangers. Characteristics of parent/s with securely attached children include reacting quickly to the child's needs, playing frequently with their children and generally being more responsive. These children tend to be more empathic later in life, exhibit better behavior overall and are less aggressive.

The adult behavior of securely attached children includes the tendency to develop trusting, long term relationships. They also appear to possess higher self-esteem, tend to seek out social inter- actions and support, are capable of and comfortable with intimate relationships and are able to share their feeling with others. Studies show individuals with a secure attachment style feel better about their marriages and relationships as adults than individuals with insecure attachment.

2. Ambivalent Attachment: These children tend to be extremely suspicious of strangers. They exhibit considerable distress when separated from parent/s but are not necessarily comforted by the return of the parent/s. The child may exhibit rejection of the parent/s or direct aggression toward them. Others describe these children as clingy and over-dependent. Research links this style of attachment to low maternal availability.

As adults, these folks have a harder time with relationships and possess insecurity toward those they are involved with. These adults as parents may cling to their young children as a source of security. In adult relationship literature, these folks are referred to sometimes as having an "Anxious Attachment Style." They are often preoccupied with their partners to the exclusion of their own interests and have difficulty focusing on anything else. There are usually undercurrents of doubt as to whether their partners will love them back and they become very anxious during separations from the partner.

3. Avoidant Attachment: These children tend to avoid their parent/s in general, with the avoidance becoming more pronounced after a period of absence. They do not seek out comfort or contact with the caregiver nor do they show a preference between a parent and a stranger.

As adults these folks have significant difficulty with relationships. They do not invest much emotion and experience little distress when the relationships end. They may have a series of shallow relationships over time and simply engage in casual sex. They are not likely to support partners during stressful times and possess an inability to share feelings, thoughts and emotions with partners.

4. Disorganized Attachment: These children exhibit a lack of any clear attachment behavior. It appears to be a mix of avoidant and ambivalent styles and these children often appear confused. Inconsistent care behavior may contribute to this as well as outright abuse. The parent is sometimes available, sometimes unavailable and sometimes terrifying. They act as both figures of fear and figures of reassurance to the child, thereby contributing to the disorganized attachment. The child feels both fear and comfort.

Attachment in Your Life Today

So how does this affect you now and what to do about it? The following is from *Attached* by Amir Levine, MD, and Rachel S.F. Heller, MA: "Adult attachment refers to how people perceive and respond to intimacy in romantic relationships. Basically, secure people feel comfortable with intimacy and are usually warm and loving; anxious people crave intimacy, are often preoccupied with their relationships and tend to worry about their partners ability to love them back; avoidant people equate intimacy with a loss of independence and constantly try to minimize closeness. In addition, people with each of these attachment styles differ in:

- Their view of intimacy and togetherness.

- The way they deal with conflict.

- Their attitude toward sex.

- Their ability to communicate their wishes and needs.

- Their expectations from their partner and the relationship."

Attachment as a relational difficulty goes back to attachment as a personal difficulty. The ability to trust and develop meaningful relationships with others is deeply rooted in your own attachment style. How you interpret others' motives and desires are fashioned by your own experiences, and how you treat the significant person in your life is also by this design. Do you push them away as you believe the inevitable parting then is under your control? Do you cling too tightly? Do you vacillate between each of these? Do you believe others are capable of loving you or meeting your needs and do you choose a person who is capable? Do you hook up with others and not really give a rat's behind when the relationship ends?

> The ability to trust and develop meaningful relationships with others is deeply rooted in your own attachment style.

What's Your Style?

So what style are you, and what style is your partner? There is no right or wrong. It just helps to know which style you are, as it will help you determine where your relationship problems may be coming from. Again, the following is taken straight from *Attached*, by Dr. Amir Levine and Rachel Heller. I strongly encourage you to read this valuable resource.

"Anxious You love to be very close to your romantic partner and have the capacity for great intimacy. You often fear, however, that your partner does not wish to be as close as you would like him/her to be. Relationships tend to consume a large part of your emotional energy. You tend to be very sensitive to small fluctuations in your partner's mood and actions, and although your senses are often accurate, you take your partner's behaviors too personally. You experience a lot of negative emotions within the relationship and get easily upset. As a result, you tend to act out and say things you later regret. If the other person provides a lot of security and reassurance, however, you are able to shed much of your preoccupation and feel contented.

Secure Being warm and loving in a relationship comes naturally to you. You enjoy being intimate without becoming overly worried about your relationships. You take things in stride when it comes to romance and don't get easily upset over relationship matters. You effectively communicate your needs and feelings to your partner and are strong at reading your partner's emotional cues and responding to them. You share your successes and problems with your mate, and are able to be there for him or her in times of need.

Avoidant It is very important for you to maintain your independence and self-sufficiency and you often prefer autonomy to intimate relationships. Even though you do want to be close to others, you feel uncomfortable with too much closeness and tend to keep your mate at arm's length. You don't spend much time worrying about your romantic relationships or about being rejected. You tend not to open up to your partners and they often complain that you are emotionally distant. In relationships, you are often on high alert for any signs of control or impingement on your territory by your partner."

15

Attention and Focus Problems

Attention Deficit Disorder (ADD) has become the new common cold. It is now found in adults, children and toddlers, and medication is typically the tool of choice in "treating" the symptoms. Those who feel distracted or cannot seem to stay on task have been told or may believe that they are suffering from Attention Deficit. This disorder does exist, but it is very overdone. There are many environmental and situational reasons why a person is having difficulty concentrating.

The typical person from a poorly run household or family also suffers these symptoms and will be anxious, conflicted and full of confusing thoughts. A person who suffers Generalized Anxiety Disorder also exhibits difficulty concentrating. Depression too carries with it the symptom of not being able to focus your attention. It's hard to pay attention when your mind is on the last terrifying or insulting and hurtful event that took place or wondering when the next one might come. A chaotic environment is not conducive to learning how to focus your mind productively. If your mind is preoccupied with scary or worrisome thoughts or feels overwhelmed, it cannot take in information and process it properly. Under those circumstances, you may read something a hundred times but feel like you have no idea what it means. Someone may repeat something to you several times and you still do not remember what was said.

This is not necessarily ADD; instead it may be anxiety. To pay attention in order to learn something, your mind has to be in relatively quiet shape. A mind that feels crazy is not one that can take in a lot of new information. This is not a learning disorder however it does affect children at school and adults at work. If you are living with a personality disordered individual, you may not be able to think straight

A chaotic environment is not conducive to learning how to focus your mind productively.

for a good part of your day as you try to sort out all the input from this person. This phenomenon is called "crazy making" in the literature.

Another less popular reason for the inability to focus is a **lack of knowledge** that this may be something under your power to control. Maybe you were just not taught that the ability to focus is a valuable skill that should be developed. Perhaps your parents didn't feel it was important or were told that your lack of focus was the result of a medical condition. Some parents believe that either you are a focused person or you're not, and that people are born with those abilities. They may not have realized that it is something that you teach and then encourage a child to practice. People are not necessarily disordered because they don't make themselves pay attention. They may not know how. Mindfulness as a tool as well as lessening the distractions in order to perform at a higher level are discussed in greater detail in Part III.

16

Boundary Issues

Boundaries are a very important part of your identity, and they actually help to define who you are. They dictate who you want to be with, what sorts of activities you find acceptable, and how you interact with others. They allow you to set schedules and keep others from intruding into your personal space. They come from having a good sense of self-worth and they are the limits that you set to let others know how you want to be treated. Boundary development requires understanding limits at two levels: (1) that you respect and do not overstep the **boundaries set by others,** and (2) that you set and enforce **your own healthy boundaries**.

Boundaries come in four identified types. Intellectual boundaries are the things you think and believe in, your ideas such as those of a political nature and the ideas and concepts that make up your knowledge base and the things you want to think about or focus on. Physical boundaries are those that explain to others about your "personal space" and how you will accept being touched or not. Emotional boundaries have to do with your emotional experience of the world and relationships and are infringed upon in verbally abusive relationships and interactions where your feelings are not considered. Spiritual boundaries define your religious or spiritual side. An extreme form of an attempt to break a spiritual boundary is when one is pushed to join a cult or religious sect.

An example of someone with a boundary difficulty is an individual who has a hard time setting limits with their family of origin and allows them to interfere with the current nuclear family. This may alienate the spouse or partner and set up chaos in the home. Parents without a proper sense of boundaries may be intrusive into the lives of their children, and they may not know what is appropriate in terms of boundaries within a marriage.

You may allow people to run all over you in relationships.

People who lack proper boundaries may also interfere in the lives of their friends, without realizing what they are doing. It is likely that they then experience rejection. They may call too late at night, invite themselves to events or the homes of others, or enter into conversations that do not concern them. The deep beliefs in these individuals usually involve fears that they may be taken advantage of, that they may become invisible or non-existent to others if not right in their face and business every moment or that they will somehow lose "control" if they back off a bit.

Other examples include letting everyone make demands of you and never saying no or setting limits for yourself that feel good. You may allow people to run all over you in relationships. You may feel forced to accept their ideas and beliefs at the cost of your own.

Boundary problems are sometimes the result of a lack of knowledge that they are necessary features in a healthy and happy life. They may never have been taught or enforced in the home. Sometimes individuals fail to form boundaries as they fear rejection if they assert themselves and their needs. They may believe that this is behaving in a selfish manner or that they will hurt others.

Whenever a boundary is broken, there is an accompanying negative emotion. It is impossible to ignore your boundaries and feel good. The most common negative emotions that you will experience if you are allowing your boundaries to be broken are anger, anxiety, depression and helplessness. You may find yourself becoming what is called "passive-aggressive" or just outright aggressive in an attempt to protect yourself and react to a perceived intrusion.

17

Caretaking

Caretaking behaviors are those which tend to keep people in a dependent sort of relationship with you. They may appear as those that come from the goodness of your heart but in reality have a lot to do with keeping others under your control. These behaviors may place you in the position of being the one that everyone turns to for help when in need; you may be seen as the foundation or "rock" that they can lean on.

They may even take the form of monetary or material gifts that have strings attached that also keep others under your control. You may take on too much responsibility for the welfare of others, disabling them from making their own decisions and taking responsibility for themselves. Along with taking too much responsibility for them, you may also set rules and standards of your own that you expect them to live by.

Caretaking behaviors also are sometimes designed to lessen the chance of misbehavior on the part of those around you or to "clean up the mess" after some less than desirable event has happened. By engaging in the "clean up," you are usually enabling individuals to continue in their own dysfunction. Those dysfunctional persons in turn fear taking responsibility for themselves or making their own decisions as that may result in rejection from the caretaker.

The Flip Side for Caretakers

As much as Caretaking might make you feel in control of things, there is a flip side. Somewhere deep down you really feel frustrated over the amount of energy and effort it takes to "help" all these people, often with no credit or reward. Relationships are meant to be "give and take." Therefore, you may feel resentment for doing all the giving, even though you are allowing it. You may find yourself becoming passive-aggressive and indirectly do or say things out of anger. If you're really stuck in this role, you may take on way too many people who take advantage or allow you to "mother" them. You may find that all your social and free time is swept up with these leeches, and you are not tending to your own interests, hobbies or things that would add joy to your life. Your self-worth can be caught up in your ability to care for others, and you may keep them around based on their neediness.

The absurdity of it is that you are usually caretaking to keep people around who you believe might otherwise not love you. But who wants them around anyway? Obviously they cannot contribute to a relationship in any meaningful manner or they wouldn't be in this mess with you. Or if you're extremely controlling, they might not be able to break free and you are thereby crippling them in their own lives. Meanwhile, it may feel "comfortable and safe" for you.

Your self-worth can be caught up in your ability to care for others.

You may not consciously think this way; it is not likely that you are out to do harm. These behaviors are usually part of an ingrained pattern that you have learned in a dysfunctional past. You may fear being alone or that no one will love you. Maybe your parents made you the "little parent" and their love was based on how well you fulfilled this role.

Often Caretakers actually take this dynamic into their careers, becoming nurses or social workers, even psychologists. That's how ingrained the pattern may be. Sometimes it makes for a wonderful nurse, other times it makes for a nurse who would prefer to be an architect. Wouldn't you rather have the nurse who really wants to be there?

18

Codependency

Codependency is one of the biggies in relationship malfunction, and it's actually a personal issue but "It takes two to tango." It is basically a fear and self-esteem issue. The term historically related to people who attached themselves to alcoholics or drug addicts. Now it has been extended to cover the gamut of bad partner qualities. It's defined as people who attach themselves or bring about relationships with individuals that are somehow needy or lacking, and they meet the needs of the individual in order to keep the individual in the relationship.

They believe that no one would stay with them just for love, so they make sure the other person somehow needs them. They might be the one who enables the person to keep being a substance abuser—covering for him/her at work or by financially taking on all the responsibility of the home. They might also be willing to put up with the person being passed out night after night. In contrast, someone with better self-esteem would demand more from the individual. Codependents will basically put up with anything for fear of losing the bad partner. In addition, they believe that they can't get a better partner.

> **Pity and rescue often get confused with love in codependent relationships.**

To clarify, if using the alcoholic scenario, the term "Codependency" is defined as one person in the relationship being dependent on alcohol and the other one being dependent on the fact that the other is dependent on alcohol. Without the alcohol, where would the relationship be? That is the fear of the codependent individual. In fact, the other person may try to kick the habit, and the codependent will sabotage the effort for fear that the person will no longer want him/her. This is also very closely tied to Caretaker behavior. These are separated so the definitions are clear.

Codependency typically refers to partner or intimate relationships, while Caretaker difficulties can be with offspring, siblings or other family members as well as with romantic partners. There are also scenarios where a caretaker will latch on to a needy neighbor or friend in order to feel needed or in control. Caretakers also typically enjoy the image that they feel their behavior creates for them, one of caring and being the person that others turn to in times of need. Although some codependents enjoy this as well and will play the martyr, it is not true of all.

Pity and rescue often get confused with love in codependent relationships. The partner typically has no sense of his/her real identity; it becomes tied in to the dysfunctional relationship.

There are many theories as to how Codependency develops. Some believe it to be a learned behavior, learned by watching your family of origin or others in their relationships. This means that you are so used to this system that to marry anyone other than an alcoholic or whatever would feel alien. Although the situation is not pleasant, it is familiar and you know how to work this system. This may be true of some, but may not be the only way these relationships develop. They also may be a product of fear, a fear that you are not lovable, no one will want you, and you are somehow unworthy of a good or healthy person.

Chronic Anger

Typically individuals know if they are angry but there are some who do not. Road rage, sarcasm, put-downs and scoffing at others or at the world in general are usually anger-based—so can be spouting off continually about politics or what is wrong with the world. Masked as citizenship, the persons may not even be in touch with where their anger is coming from or even that they are angry. Those who believe they are right and everybody else is wrong are difficult to be around.

Chronic anger is toxic, to the individuals experiencing it and to everyone in their world. It usually begins in childhood or early adulthood as a response to helplessness, abuse, being insulted or bullied in some way or just because bad things happened. Maybe it was a loss of a parent, parents who left the person mad at the world, or a god who he/she believes to be unjust. With no real target or solution to the cause, the anger comes out everywhere. When you combine anger and control, you get individuals who may become bullies themselves. They fear venting their anger where it belongs, and instead they take it out on a more vulnerable individual or group. It's not unusual for them to come into every situation expecting the worst or at least a confrontation from someone.

If you aren't sure if this is you, ask someone close to you, and be ready for his/her response. Don't kill the messenger, but rather accept the information to move forward.

Studies show anger as the unhealthiest emotion, apparently releasing hormones or chemicals into the bloodstream that are considered "sticky." Those "sticky" chemicals like to adhere to the arteries, making it more likely to develop a blockage, possibly resulting in heart disease or stroke. Anger can block the ability to fully connect with others or to enjoy healthy relationships. Chronic anger typically blocks any ability to experience joy.

> **Anger can block the ability to fully connect with others or to enjoy healthy relationships.**

Thinking styles and inner language tend to promote anger without you even realizing it. These thinking styles are called *attributions*, and the name given for the phenomenon is *Attribution Theory*, i.e. how you perceive an event, not the event itself, is how you will react. If you perceive that someone has slighted you, even if the person didn't, you will become angry and behave as though they did. Sometimes you have expectations of others, and when they don't meet those expectations, you become angry.

This is covered in more depth in Part III.

20

Depression

Depression has the power to rob you of all possible joy, and suffering from any form of depression can affect all areas of your life. Family life, productivity, career and social relationships become caught up in the downward spiral of mood and energy and render you feeling helpless. Not surprisingly, depression is one of the most common symptoms shared by adults who come from abusive or dysfunctional homes. Who wouldn't be sad if they had been physically or sexually abused, made to feel like they didn't matter, or if they had never laughed and played without fear as a child? Of course, a child who has been abandoned or lives with the threat of abandonment develops a depression and grief response.

Depression is a natural reaction if you are never validated as an individual, are ridiculed regularly for what you're thinking, are called names, or live through endless put-downs or tirades of negativity. Feelings of helplessness actually translate into depression. Interestingly, it is possible to see the same helpless response in children from all the family types discussed in Part I of this book.

Genetically and/or Biologically Based?

It's very difficult to prove whether depression has any actual familial or genetic links, as you have to factor in thinking patterns of the parents that are passed down from generation to generation as well as personal circumstances such as abuse. If you are taught negative or pessimistic thinking patterns, you will most likely think this way also. Yet it is not because it was passed to you like hair color.

"Bad chemicals," such as cortisol, can take over the "good chemicals," such as serotonin and dopamine, which are needed for mood stability.

A very common belief today is that there are **chemical imbalances** in the brain that cause depression. However, there are conflicting theories as to whether you are born that way or whether chronic stress, environment, poor diet and worry produce the "bad chemicals." These "bad chemicals," such as cortisol, can take over the "good chemicals," such as serotonin and dopamine, which are needed for mood stability.

There are some illnesses and medical conditions that can cause medical depression, including hypothyroidism, some heart conditions, and hormonal imbalances (more so in women). **True Bipolar Depression** is also a very serious medical condition requiring treatment. Substance abuse can alter blood sugar levels and brain chemicals, thereby affecting moods. Some medications such as birth control and hormone treatments are also capable of producing depressive symptoms.

A Look at Three of the Major Types

There are different types of depression. The three most common ones are defined here: Major Depressive Disorder, Dysthymia and Bipolar Depression.

Major Depression or Major Depressive Disorder is characterized by a combination of symptoms that interfere with the individual's ability to function normally in academic, work or social settings. Typically there are symptoms of sleeplessness or too much sleep, appetite irregularities with weight gain or loss, fatigue, sensitivity, irritability and crying spells. Sadness and feelings of hopelessness are also typically involved. There is a loss of interest in activities and perhaps in appearance and hygiene. In extreme cases, thoughts of suicide may be present.

Dysthymia is a long-term sort of depression, whereby the individual feels sad more often than not. Though it may continue for many years, this disorder doesn't normally involve suicidal thoughts. The chronically depressed mood on most days lasts at least two years. In children, this may appear as irritability. During these two years, if the person does become symptom-free, it typically doesn't last more than two months. For a formal diagnosis, the depressive symptoms must cause clinically significant impairment in social, occupational or other important areas of functioning.

Bipolar Depression or Manic Depression is a very serious mood disorder. These individuals alternate between periods of depression and what is called *Mania*, or a state of what appears to be elation. There are two types, *Bipolar I* that involves Mania or mixed episodes of Depression and Mania, and what is called *Bipolar II* that involves what is called a *Hypomanic Episode*.

The main difference between Manic and Hypomanic is that the individual experiencing a Hypomanic Episode does not lose touch with reality, whereas a person in a Mania typically does. They may be visually hallucinating, hearing voices or be experiencing delusions and extremely unrealistic thoughts such as, "I am going to sit on this sofa and make it fly." A person who is Bipolar I or Bipolar II requires medical monitoring, although the individual can certainly benefit from counseling and talk therapies to manage the symptoms.

Other Considerations

For the last 20 years, **Bipolar Disorder** has become very over-diagnosed. Just mood swings or periods of irritability can bring about a diagnosis. Grumpy husbands have been diagnosed with Bipolar by their wives. It is being diagnosed in infants and children, which was historically unheard of. It was believed that, prior to late adolescence and young adulthood, you would not see a real episode of Bipolar Disorder, similar to Schizophrenia. Borderline Personality Disorder is also commonly mistaken for Bipolar Disorder, due to the rapid mood swings and seeming instability.

You may feel many of the symptoms listed above and still not meet the criteria for a clinically diagnosed depression or mood disorder. A major life event may have left you reeling in its wake or you may just feel a pervasive sadness that is difficult to shake. You may be experiencing isolation and loneliness, resulting from a move or an illness. Despite the lack of a formal diagnosis, the symptoms can certainly be harsh enough for you to want to eradicate them from your life.

Depression can certainly affect your relationships. The most obvious is that if you are depressed, you won't be functioning at your optimal best. You may not be pulling your weight in the relationship, and if it has been a long time, your partner may be tired of carrying the extra burden. Not to mention that a depressed person is not much fun to be around, unless you hide it really well. It often impacts your sexual desire negatively, as well as your desire to do things or go places. You may be heavily medicated and unable to drive or take care of your children. You may be on worker's compensation, thereby creating financial difficulty for the family.

As a chronically depressed person, you may have attracted a depressed mate, thereby making your own recovery harder. You may have attracted a codependent, someone who is invested in keeping you depressed to meet his/her own needs. Depressive symptoms do not necessarily only affect partner and family relationships; they may hurt your friendships, relationships with co-workers, etc. Depression has a way of creeping into all aspects of your life.

> **Depression is one of the most common symptoms shared by adults who come from abusive or dysfunctional homes.**

21

Hypervigilance or "Boy Scout Brain"

Hypervigilance is typically related to anxiety. However, given the number of individuals who experience it, I am giving it its own section. Hypervigilant individuals are never able to relax. Not that they don't want to relax; their brain just doesn't allow it to happen. This too is a normal reaction to chaos or uncertainty in the environment. You are geared for survival. If your brain becomes hypervigilant, it means it is working properly if not overtime to ensure your survival. It's always on the lookout (hence the term "Boy Scout") for potential danger so you will be ready to react. Picture a few soldiers on your forehead doing lookout if this helps.

Boy Scout Brain usually develops in your family of origin, and can carry over to your entire life. It also often develops in reaction to a death, accident or some other terrible event that affected you or your loved ones. You may always be on the lookout for personal harm, partner validation, environmental disaster, a plane crash, etc. People who work in high stress jobs, like police officers, firefighters, emergency crews and soldiers, often experience this as well. It may or may not have developed in early life for them.

Often individuals with hypervigilant qualities become very con-trolling; they feel that they are then protecting themselves and/or loved ones from potential disasters. They try to stay one step ahead of the next threat. *Whew!! What a job!* Being on the lookout means you have to pay attention, making it hard to relax or focus on other things. Parents who are hypervigilant may warn their children constantly not to do this or that, for fear of the many dangers it may present. Thereby, they can instill in the child a fear of the world in general. These

Often individuals with hypervigilant qualities become very controlling.

children are often not allowed to participate in activities the parent deems dangerous or out of control.

Hypervigilant individuals are typically the ones that favor the aisle seats in any circumstance, and they like to face the doors, as opposed to having their back to them. They don't want to feel that there is no escape. It is not uncommon for them to back their cars into parking spaces in order to be able to get out quickly if need be.

22

Learned Helplessness

This is huge. It is a psychological state in which individuals have learned to believe that they are helpless in particular situations. The individual feels that they have no control and "give up." The result is that they have learned to remain passive in the face of unpleasant, harmful or damaging circumstances, even when they actually have the power to change things. It is further defined as the "giving up reaction" or "quitting response" that follows from the belief that whatever you do doesn't matter or doesn't change things.

Learned helplessness is closely related to your explanatory style or *Locus of Control*, which is discussed next. Much research has been done in this area over the years, and it has repeatedly reported links to emotional ills. It's easy to see how Learned Helplessness can lead to dependency, anxiety, pessimism, depression and despair.

As adults with free choice, you are never helpless.

As a child, you may not have been able to escape the dysfunction you were subjected to—whether it was physical or emotional. You may have felt that no matter how hard you tried to be "good," you were still punished. This was due to your family's dysfunction and should be left at their door. As adults with free choice, you are never helpless. If you are being abused currently, you can leave as there are a myriad of help systems in place. It may be scary and hard, as you may not have the same financial resources in a new situation. Still, you have the choice to leave. If your children are being abused, you have an obligation to remove them from the situation. You are not helpless.

In psychological treatment, Learned Helplessness theory is the idea that depression and related emotional illness can result from the perceived absence of control over personal situations. Therapists then help the individuals develop the necessary thought processes and beliefs that allow them to see where their behaviors and decisions are actually important and do determine their outcomes. This instills hope in individuals in that they now will be designing their own future. It brings with it a certain amount of excitement and new enthusiasm toward life in general.

23

Locus of Control

This concept is also huge in matters of mental health, and it defines how you approach almost everything in life. This is a concept you need to get down cold. It is a thinking style that refers to how you perceive the cause of life's events. Do you believe that your destiny is controlled by you or by external forces, such as luck, chance or fate? An unproductively focused Locus of Control is very closely tied to depression and hopelessness.

The Two Types
There are thought to be two types of Locus of Control:

> **1. Internal Locus of Control:** This is the belief that your outcomes are contingent on what you do to make them happen—*your own decisions and efforts.* You tend to accept responsibility as well as credit for your actions. This orientation has been shown to generate more effort and willingness to take risk, as well as being behind high motivation and perseverance. The thinking is … *"If good things happen, I deserve credit for my hard work or abilities. If something bad happens, it's due to something I did wrong or could have done better."*

2. External Locus of Control: This is the belief that your outcomes are contingent on events outside your control (again, due to luck, chance or fate). When bad things happen or you behave in a poor fashion, you tend not to take ownership of it. The thinking is … "The government was late with my check. It wasn't my fault I needed money and overdrew my checking account." On the flip side, if something good happens or you are successful at something, you take no ownership of that either (i.e., if you get a job you wanted, you assume that there were no other candidates or the employer was in a hurry to hire someone).

In general, it is considered to be more psychologically healthy to possess a certain level of *Internal Locus of Control.*

Note that Locus of Control is largely a *learned* concept. It may be a response to circumstances, and in the case of toxic environments, it is easy to see where this may go haywire. In general, people with a more Internal Locus of Control tend to have better paying jobs, be more achievement-oriented, and more resilient in the face of adversity.

> **It is considered to be more psychologically healthy to possess a certain level of *Internal Locus of Control.***

Perhaps you have been told that you have no ability or are no good and worthless. Chances are you then did not develop Internal Locus of Control. The thinking is … "If something good happened, it must be due to luck as I have no ability."

If you were never held to task for actual bad behavior, you may have developed an *External Locus of Control.* If you do not take responsibility for something you have done, you may instead attribute it to be someone else's fault or just attribute it to bad luck.

Taking responsibility for bad behavior means you attribute it to a bad choice on your part and know that you can make better choices. You have then internalized the responsibility and the behavior. With an External Locus of Control, you may also have developed a sense of entitlement. Your ego may not be able to handle the thought of a mistake or failure of some sort. This usually stems from a deep seated feeling of insecurity and inferiority.

Locus of Control is a teachable concept that will open up the world to you. You might think this sounds too simple, but it's not. This, combined with some of the other concepts to be discussed, is all you're going to need to approach

It will feel good to be armed with the tools to be in control of your life.

the world in a whole new way. It will feel good to be armed with the tools to be in control of your life.

24

Low Self-Esteem

Self–esteem is the term used to describe a person's own measurement of his/her self-worth. It is how you think of yourself, describe yourself and the collection of beliefs you have pertaining to your abilities and worthiness. The evaluations you make can be positive as in "I am a good person" or negative as in "I am stupid." These beliefs are typically held regardless of any evidence being present; they merely represent what you think or believe to be true. Your self-esteem often dictates how you treat yourself or how you allow others to treat you.

Not surprisingly, depressed individuals normally have relatively poor self-esteem. Anxious individuals typically worry constantly about performance and other issues, suggesting that they also suffer low or troubled self-esteem.

> **Self-esteem affects how you think, feel and make decisions in matters that relate to you.**

Self-Esteem is not a temperament quality or other quality that you inherit from your genetic background. It is usually a learned belief derived from information given you from your surroundings or your interpretation of the information. Abusive parents almost always produce children with low self-esteem as do critical or overly judgmental ones. Individuals from abandoning type families often have poor self-esteem as reflected in their attachment behavior as well as overall functioning.

Self-esteem includes the concepts of self-confidence and self-respect. Self-confidence may have to do with the capacity to perform some activity or task. Self-respect involves a feeling of personal worth, which leads individuals to treat themselves well, take care of themselves, and believe that they have the right to be happy and be loved. The importance of self-esteem is that it influences how you behave and interpret the world around you, including others. Self-esteem affects how you think, feel and make decisions in matters that relate to you.

Characteristics of High and Low Self-Esteem

Positive self-esteem possesses the following characteristics:

1. **Believing in a set of firmly placed values and principles** and being able to defend or assert yourself in the face of opposition to them. If after learning something new, the old value does not fit, individuals with positive self-esteem do not have difficulty modifying the belief.

2. **Being able to make choices,** trust your own judgment, and not feel guilty about choices if someone does not agree.

3. **Not living in the past or future,** not worrying about "what if's." Living fully in the present.

4. **Believing in your capacity to solve problems,** adjust to failures, and ask for assistance.

5. **Participating in and enjoying** many activities and hobbies.

6. **Believing that you are valuable,** and that others will enjoy spending time with you.

7. Resisting manipulation by others.

8. Being sensitive to the feelings and needs of others; accept and abide by social norms.

9. Considering yourself self-worthy and equal to others, regardless of differences in finance and personal success.

In contrast, **low self-esteem** is characterized by:

1. Heavy self criticism, tending to create a habitual state of dissatisfaction with yourself. Exaggerating the magnitude of mistakes or behaviors and not able to reach self forgiveness.

2. Hypersensitivity to criticism leading to feeling attacked and not being open to constructive criticism.

3. Chronic indecision due to fear of making mistakes.

4. Excessive will to please out of fear of displeasing someone.

5. Perfectionism, which leads to constant frustration or underachievement when perceived perfection is not achieved.

6. Hostility or irritability—easily angered even over minor things.

7. Feelings of insignificance.

8. General negativity about life and often an inability to enjoy life.

Given the characteristics above, it is easy to see the

> **Self-esteem includes the concepts of self-confidence and self-respect.**

commonalities in depression and poor self-esteem. Treating a poor self-esteem works wonders for depressed individuals. Challenging yourself, changing your focus, and learning some better thinking skills can boost self-esteem almost immediately.

25

Personality Disorders

Personality disorders are enduring behavior patterns that are usually developed in young adulthood or before, and they can be very difficult to treat. They're not just single behaviors but rather a pattern that remains quite constant and deviates from the norm. It is usually apparent to others that these individuals are "different" in some way; they behave in ways that are not typical.

Their interpretations and perceptions of events and of interpersonal relations differ quite a bit from the rest of society. Their emotional responses to things are sometimes too intense or lacking in sincerity or just lacking, period. The

> **Emotional responses to things are sometimes too intense or lacking in sincerity or just lacking.**

behaviors typically cause distress and impairment across settings and one reason they are difficult to treat is that the individuals typically lack insight into their own behavior and motivations.

Borderline Personality Disorder, Antisocial Personality Disorder, Dependent Personality Disorder, Narcissistic Personality Disorder, and Histrionic Personality Disorder are the most common and it is likely that you have encountered these individuals somewhere along the line. If you are from an abusive family, it is almost a guarantee that you have encountered one. Personality disorders are a science in themselves, and this is not an exhaustive description but rather general information to familiarize oneself with the concepts.

Borderline Personality Disorder is typically seen in females and can be seen as early as adolescence. These individuals are very volatile in mood, and their moods can shift rapidly—happy one minute and angry the next.

This disorder is sometimes misdiagnosed as Bipolar Disorder due to these mood swings, which typically are fast and can shift many times during a day. However, the bipolar individual is typically shifting mood due to some shift in brain function and chemicals whereas a Borderline Personality Disordered person's moods shift due to something that has happened and the individual perceives it improperly. Usually the events that have occurred threaten the person's security or relationship in some way.

Borderlines make frantic efforts to avoid being abandoned, whether it is real or imagined and these efforts may involve suicidal threats and/or attempts. They often have great difficulty with impulse control and may go on major shopping sprees, drive recklessly or be promiscuous. Their interpersonal relations are usually maintained at a shallow level as they have not developed a real sense of self. They may be a lot of fun to be with initially but their relationships tend to suffer due to their moods and demandingness. It is likely that they call others with many crises and have poor boundaries. There has usually been a pattern throughout their life of unstable and perhaps very intense relationships.

It is not uncommon for Borderlines to love their partner intensely one minute and hate them the next. They can exhibit extreme anger and have difficulty controlling this anger. Sometimes this anger and emotional pain is directed inward and they may engage in "cutting" or harming themselves but not with the intent to commit suicide.

Antisocial Personality Disorder is what our prisons are full of. These individuals have a pattern starting quite early in life of disregarding and violating the rights of others. They commit crimes repeatedly and show no regard for authority or our laws as a society. Deceitfulness and a lack of impulse control are a way of life. They may not hold jobs for long and can be irresponsible financially. If they hurt someone, there is no remorse other than if they get caught and suffer consequences. They will rationalize their behavior or turn it around to look like you did something to them. "My grandmother wouldn't let me use the car so I had to kill her. I really needed the car." Their own needs always come first and there is a chronic disregard for the safety of others.

Dependent Personality Disorder is defined as the pervasive and excessive need to be taken care of that leads to submissive and clinging behavior and fears of separation, beginning by early adulthood and present across life contexts. These individuals exhibit difficulty making everyday decisions and require a great deal of advice and reassurance from those around them. They may ask wait staff for help with the menu in restaurants, salespeople for excessive help in buying clothing, etc. They will rarely disagree with others for fear of the loss of support and approval, even engaging in activities that are harmful or unpleasant in order not to lose this support. This includes those who allow their children to be abused.

These individuals tend to move directly from one relationship into another as they fear being on their own. They are in fact quite obsessed with the idea that they cannot care for themselves. They tend to have great difficulty initiating projects, careers or anything else on their own due to this extreme lack of self-confidence.

Narcissistic Personality Disorder is exhibited as a pervasive pattern of grandiosity, need for admiration, and lack of empathy. These individuals have a great opinion of themselves that includes exaggerated achievements and talents. Being "special" is important. They expect to be recognized and treated as special individuals and are often preoccupied with fantasies of unlimited success and power or beauty. They may or may not actually be very successful and require excessive admiration and will reject others if they feel it is not forthcoming. A sense of entitlement is in place and they feel they should be treated differently from others. Typically their expectations for favorable treatment are unreasonable. In relationships they are unable to experience empathy and will ignore the feelings of others. They may exploit the relationships in order to achieve their own goals.

Histrionic Personality Disorder. These are the true "Theater People," and are defined as exhibiting excessive emotionality and attention seeking, beginning by early adulthood and present in a variety of life contexts. They *have to be* the center of attention and are not comfortable or are bored in situations where they are not. They may use their appearance to draw attention to themselves and exhibit great dramatization and exaggerated expression while engaged in conversation. They may be very seductive or provocative. They may also interpret relationships as being more intimate than they actually are.

These are the true "Theater People."

For instance, if they meet you once, they will later describe you to someone else as being "their best friend." Finally, these individuals tend to be very impressionable themselves and can be easily influenced by others. They usually have some crises going on around them and may stir something up if there is not as they glean satisfaction from all the attention these crises bring them. It is exhausting for those in relationships with the Histrionics as there is this never ending upheaval. It is usually their very charm and expressiveness that draws others into relationships with them. They too, like the Borderlines, can be a great deal of fun initially.

26

Poor Coping Strategies

Poor coping strategies are those that you engage in to make yourself feel better or to buffer yourself from the outside world of stressors that are bothering you. They make you feel good for the moment but typically create bigger problems the longer you indulge in them. These can develop in relation to all the dysfunctional parenting styles as you seek to alleviate your emotional distress.

Poor coping strategies can be relatively benign or can be horrendous in terms of robbing you of quality of life, such as drug or alcohol addiction. Binge eating or overeating in general damages your health and appearance. All of these lead to further loss of self-esteem if you had any to start with.

Retail therapy or chronic shopping, whether or not you have the financial means to pay for things, is another buffer. Buying that new item, car or whatever feels great in the moment while you are doing it, as it focuses you on a project for the time being. However, when all is said and done, you have another item of clothing or jewelry or a new car and that is it. Maybe you also have a bill coming in next month or more payments added to your monthly budget. Plus it won't be long before the urge to do it again takes over and gives you that good feeling once more.

Those are the obvious poor coping strategies, but there are others just as damaging to yourself and to your potential relationships. One poor coping strategy that many are unaware of—persons who get "sick" with physical ailments, depression, whatever, requiring a lot of care and attention. The gain here is that these individuals believe no one will leave them while they are sick and they get lots of attention! They are a victim. Worse, they may make out that their children are "sick" with behavior problems, attention deficit, whatever, thereby also getting a lot of attention from doctors and therapists and friends and family, being the care-taker of sick children, or a martyr.

> **Buying that new item, car or whatever feels great in the moment.**

Other coping strategies that are poor choices are promiscuity, before or during marriage. This happens as the individual seeks love in all the wrong places. Sexually abused individuals typically see their worth tied up in their sexuality and use it to gain "love and acceptance." They are doing what they have been taught in a way. However, it is still a poor and often dangerous choice and needs to be unlearned. Individuals may cheat in their marriage as a means to continue to feel loved when the initial spark of the marriage dies down. They may fear their partner is on the way out the door and they should be "shopping for the next one." Some people just use sex the same as drugs or alcohol; it feels good while they're doing it and blots out the emotional pain they may be experiencing for a while.

> **Everything is not a "disorder;" some behaviors are just poor choices or lapses in judgment.**

Sex addiction is the new term for this. Possibly it is a defensive term for a poor coping strategy or a lack of self-discipline. Generating excitement and proving over and over that you are desirable by engaging in constant sexual "conquests" is just a poor way to feel good about yourself. These folks are often "adrenaline junkies" and love the thrill that the new experiences create. Everything is not a "disorder;" some behaviors are really just poor choices or lapses in judgment.

Becoming a *workaholic* is sometimes also a coping strategy. If your mind is

The opposite of workaholism is becoming a *basket case* in order to avoid growing up, as you fear you can't handle it.

busy on business, it's not thinking about uncomfortable things. If this is channeled properly, it can be a good strategy. It can be listed under poor coping strategies in its pathological form, where family and life are ignored as the individual focuses primarily on work and is gone excessively from the home or emotionally absent while bodily present with family. These individuals may also fail to formulate social lives or appropriate outlets for recreation.

The opposite of workaholism is becoming a *basket case* in order to avoid growing up, as you fear you can't handle it. This individual refuses to keep jobs or sabotages jobs in order to get fired, makes a disaster of finances, may abuse substances also, and just never seems to get it together. They usually have family or friends that take care of them in some form or rescue them. They like the feeling of being rescued as it equates to love.

Being rescued prevents them from having to grow up, which is scary to them, and would require decision-making, which is what they're afraid to do.

If they're a "loser" by choice, no one can see them when they really "fail" while they're actually trying. This fear is not the motive behind everyone who exhibits these symptoms. Some people are just plain lazy and deviant, and they will take advantage of others.

If you have a person like this in your life or if *you* are the person like this, it needs to be dealt with.

27

Relationship Problems

Relationship problems come in all forms and can develop from any of the dysfunctional styles of parenting. Anyone can experience difficulty in their personal relationships from time to time, but the focus here is on individuals who are chronically involved in poor relationships, whether due to their own behavior in the relationship or just by choosing the wrong partner time and again. This just pertains to intimate relationships, but there are yet others who find themselves always at odds with colleagues, friends and social peers or even with their own children.

Not knowing how a healthy relationship works and what the expected roles or norms are is one difficulty that people from dysfunctional homes face. But if individuals don't realize that they lack this knowledge, they may revolve in and out of relationships always blaming the other person for the resulting disaster. If you have been exposed to an abusive relationship of any sort, you may tend to choose partners that mirror the exact qualities of your dysfunctional parent. There are theories that suggest that individuals choose this way, consciously or subconsciously as these are the dynamics that they understand and know how to deal with as they did it their entire young lives. These dynamics almost feel "comfortable." However, it leaves you facing a life of abuse and repeating the cycle with your own children.

You have seen or maybe are the person who dates or marries someone who is somehow not quite up to par or whom others would not expect to be a good match. This can tie into many of the other issues such as self esteem. Sometimes you feel if you choose someone not so great it won't matter when you break up, as you try to soften the blow of the expected end of the relationship at some point. You then tell yourself that person wasn't so great anyway, no real loss.

If you have become controlling, caretaking or codependent due to self-esteem issues, you will choose someone who will enter into these types of relationships with you. These relationships don't stand a chance, particularly when one of the individuals then becomes more emotionally healthy. The same goes if you choose a depressed partner at a time when you are depressed. Chances are if you become well, the other person's depression is going to feel heavy.

> The "white knight" may come along and appear to be your salvation.

If you have developed dependent qualities or are unsure of yourself as in the invalidating or controlling families, the "white knight" may come along and appear to be your salvation. However, the white knight is typically a controlling sort who "rescues" in order to feed his own self-esteem or to establish control of the relationship.

This dynamic is typically seen in male–female relationships where the white knight is male and the damsel in distress is female. She may be a financial mess or a single mother and the assistance that is offered is welcome at the time and seemingly heaven sent. What usually plays out is that as the damsel gets herself together she begins to resent the control exerted by the knight. She begins to exert her own wishes in the relationship and exhibit independent behaviors like going out with friends and the knight then has difficulty handling that and no longer feels needed or loved.

If you don't know yourself very well when you choose a partner, chances are you will have difficulties at some point. This typically happens when people marry young or if they just accept the first offer to come along, believing it may be the only one they will receive. These couples tend to drift apart as they have little in common. They may have different values, beliefs and even child rearing ideas. Although the relationship may not be ideal, these couples can sometimes make things work out through counseling and being able to pursue their own interests within the marriage or partnership.

If you are lacking in the ability to trust others, you may always be on the lookout for them to cross you somehow. If you are interpreting their every move as having negative consequences for you, you will treat them accordingly. If your paranoia is overboard, the colleague, friend or social contact will move away from you as you are not going to be very pleasant to be around. This has to do with your attributions.

You will also experience relationship problems with others if your personality is not fully developed to be the best it can be. Unknowingly you may be exhibiting behaviors that are turning others away from you. You may not be pulling your weight in a certain relationship or you may be breaking others' boundaries, causing them not to want to be with you.

28

Trust Issues

The development of trust issues is common in any of the forms of dysfunctional homes. Whether you are being abused in some fashion, fear losing a parent's love, fear being abandoned or told constantly that your ideas are ridiculous, you come to believe that other humans are not very trustworthy with your emotional life. This tends to generalize out to all humans as the belief is "if your parents do this why wouldn't others?" After all, your parents are supposed to be the best humans in your lives in your childhood years; they are the very ones you are supposed to be able to trust. Trust issues can also be related to attachment problems as they both are outcomes of the interactions and expected outcomes of relating to others.

Perhaps you experienced infidelity in a past relationship and now expect a new partner to be a cheater. You feel that if you expect this you will not be blindsided if it happens again. But obviously it is still painful and not trusting your new partner will only bring further relationship problems. You waste time and expend much emotional energy attempting to thwart your new partner's behavior or find it to begin with. Think of how you are feeling as you are searching through the phone records or email, looking for evidence of his/her misdeeds. Maybe you come right out and accuse your partner of cheating with no evidence at all, which results in starting a fight and pushing the person away.

Trust issues can be found hand in hand with many of the other mentioned difficulties. Although commonly identified by clients as a problem, it is not always clear to them how trust issues relate to the other themes in their lives. Lack of

> **When someone has betrayed you or when you expect to be betrayed, you may behave in an angry manner or carry anger with you into all situations.**

trust can be seen as causing anxiety, in relationships and in general. It's depressing when due to a lack of trust you have excluded yourself from social interactions or developing an intimate relationship with a potentially great partner. When someone has betrayed you or when you expect to be betrayed, you may behave in an angry manner or carry anger with you into all situations. You get a big chip on your shoulder that you have been treated unfairly by someone and you aren't going to let that happen again!

Trust to some degree is a necessary piece of humanity. It allows peace of mind in certain situations and allows you to let down your guard for the moment. Remember "Boy Scout Brain"? Without some element of trust, fear rules your life.

> **Trust to some degree is a necessary piece of humanity.**

You need to be discerning in who you trust and how much to trust, but you cannot face the world alone with no one to trust.

29

Underachievement

This topic is another one that is relatively self-explanatory. Yet it is one of the biggest reasons people find themselves unhappy and unfulfilled. They don't trust their own abilities and strengths, and instead find themselves trudging through life with no direction that fits their personality. These individuals are typically characterized by poor self-esteem and a lack of purpose. Unsure of their capabilities, they may resist trying to achieve due to a fear of failure. They may have experienced some type of failure in the past and see any future attempts as futile, thereby exhibiting an overall pessimistic view of their future.

The belief that they will continue to experience a never-ending pattern of defeat is dominant. It is seen in their choice of schools, careers, friends and partners. They may be so fearful of the world around them that they don't even try to do anything other than what is required to get through the day. Or, they may

> **Underachieving individuals are typically characterized by poor self-esteem and a lack of purpose.**

be so depressed that they don't even feel like trying. Attention problems may contribute and keep them unfocused. They typically lack focus and persistence. There are a myriad of reasons people underachieve, and they are for the most part listed in the sections above, as any or all of these difficulties can stand in the way of success.

Often when underachieving individuals look in the mirror, they see or label themselves in a negative fashion. Their insecurity keeps them limited to experiences where they feel comfortable or in control. They may have a very fragile ego that has been splintered by negative interactions with family or others. They may have been told that they are stupid or incapable and therefore do not believe in their abilities that are clear to others.

Teens may not have been taught to set goals or to look toward the future, just living day-to-day and not making plans or setting a path.

Sometimes a deeply psychological issue is not the problem at all in underachievers. In teens particularly, they may not have been taught to set goals or to look toward the future, just living day-to-day and not making plans or setting a path. They are not aware that this is a helpful toolset and that achieving goals no matter what they are feels good. If parents do not teach this, it is sometimes not learned. It's easy to label a teen as an attitude or behavior problem when underachieving, but it may be just as easy to teach him or her to set goals. Everyone likes to feel good about him or herself and accomplishing things is a good way to achieve this feeling.

Tasks for Part II

At this point, you're likely to have an idea of the family pattern in which you were raised and perhaps what type of pattern your parents experienced as well. You may be able to see where some of your own unhappiness began and are able to identify the specific issues bothering you today. Make a list of those issues at this point, and under each, describe how they are causing you current distress. It helps to be clear as you move through the program outlined in Part III on the exact things you're looking to change or types of pain you're looking to alleviate.

This exercise should then look like this when complete (the *italics* represent examples of possible responses):

1. My Family Pattern (from previous task):
Histrionic Mother and Depressive Father

2. My Issues:
Anxiety, depression, attention problems, disorganized lifestyle, low self-esteem, learned helplessness

3. How These Issues Affect Me:
- *Anxiety is keeping me from feeling comfortable. I have hot flashes, an upset stomach and can't sleep well. I feel panicked at times.*
- *Depression is zapping my energy and I feel sad all the time.*
- *Attention problems are causing me to not perform well at work or school.*
- *My disorganized lifestyle leads to a messy house that causes me stress. I am always late and can't find things when I need them.*
- *Low self-esteem keeps me in a poor relationship and in a low paying job, as I don't believe I can do better.*
- *Learned helplessness keeps me from drawing boundaries with my mother, as I feel that there is nothing I can do to stop her intrusiveness. This leads to further depression, anxiety and low self-esteem.*

4. What Have I Done to Address These Issues or Feel Better in the Past?

- *I went to therapy for a few sessions, didn't feel that it helped so I quit going.*

- *I took antidepressant medication prescribed by a family doctor.*

Now it's your turn. Write down the four questions and answer them.

PART three

The Program

> "Behold the turtle. He makes progress only when he sticks his neck out." —James Conant

You are now ready to begin learning and implementing the *Dysfunction Interrupted* program itself. You have a good idea of what your thinking patterns and issues may be, and you're ready to start moving in a "feel better" direction. The steps are not difficult, but they may be very new to you. Just move through them at your own pace and take your time, paying attention to how you feel as you add each new skill set.

Most report that the first emotion they start to feel is hope. This is very positive in that it gives them the motivation to move further into the plan. And that includes you. Hope and optimism are what keep moving you through your days with a degree of satisfaction and contentment.

Excitement is often the next emotion you will feel as you begin your journey through the *Dysfunction Interrupted* program and experience the immediate improvements that come about in your life. The new found feeling of control over your destiny and the knowledge that you're designing your own life and thoughts according to your own desires is exhilarating.

Within are the nine Steps of the program. Read through each and complete the Tasks at the end of each Step before proceeding to the next—some ask you a question to "remember when ..." Others might send you to the library in search of a favorite topic. Each Task is essential to feeling better.

Now, start with Step 1, but don't wait on the Step 1 Tasks because ... they integrate with the next Step. And, one last thought: *in order to feel better immediately, you'll have to begin to implement the Steps immediately.* You may not feel that all the Steps apply to you, but I encourage you to at least read them anyway. They might surprise you. They may also apply to others you know and help you to understand them or give them guidance.

If you are feeling overwhelmed, get stuck or don't understand something, remember that coaching, answers to emailed questions and other resources are available at *DysfunctionInterrupted.com* or *PsychSkills.com.*

In This Section

Self-Soothing

*"The greatest discovery of our generation
is that human beings can alter their lives
by altering their attitudes of mind. As you
think, so shall you be."*

—WILLIAM JAMES

The first technique that is required to master any of the emotional difficulties you may encounter is one called *self-soothing*. The idea of this is so simple you'll be asking, "How is something so simple going to help me overcome depression?" Or anxiety or whatever it is you're dealing with now. Self-soothing involves the ability to manipulate your mood by calming or comforting yourself in the face of negative emotions. Simply put, it means to learn to comfort yourself without drugs, food, alcohol or other destructive distractions. It's a strategy or technique designed to help you cope with overwhelmingly negative or anxiety-provoking feelings and situations.

This is not a new concept or one of "psychological mumbo jumbo." Rather, it's what emotionally successful people learned from childhood that you might have missed, especially if you came from a dysfunctional home. It's a critical skill base geared toward self-preservation that actually can make the difference between a successful and happy individual and a deeply suffering and "stuck" person. I don't believe self-soothing has received enough atten-tion given how important it truly is. And it *is* doable for all of us.

> **Self-Soothing means to learn to comfort yourself without drugs, food, alcohol or other destructive distractions.**

Again, this is simply a skill base of techniques to use when you're feeling low. Look at it like you would to learn manners or formal etiquette; you were taught or you were not. If you weren't, you had to pick things up and learn on your own in order to prevent humiliation or embarrassment. With self-soothing, you're learning to prevent destructive behaviors and the rumination that keeps you feeling poorly. Once you learn how to self-soothe, you have the knowledge for life. Never again do you have to suffer like you did before this was part of your life's set of tools.

A New Healthy Alternative

There are days and perhaps periods of time when things may not be quite as you had hoped. As a result, you feel poorly. To be blunt, you may actually feel like absolute crap, and you're not alone. There are actually blogs with titles like "Why Do I Feel Like Crap?" You may be thinking about current or past difficulties or dreading upcoming events which would normally trigger self-destructive behaviors. You might be very anxious and fearing the next panic attack or could be experiencing an upheaval in your personal rela-tionships. You may be fearful that you are going to be abandoned by a spouse or significant other. All of these are the times when you will be most likely to gravitate back to dysfunctional habits.

You may feel like you absolutely cannot tolerate whatever it is you are feeling, and that thought alone will send you to the medicine chest, the liquor store or the Twinkie bin. You may head out on the town to find a replacement for the loved one, someone to make you feel "special and loved." Anything to thwart the pain. Unfortunately, you end up fat, drunk, zoned out or in another bad relationship. The result is more distress than you felt before setting out to make yourself feel better.

Self-soothing techniques are those you learn in order to replace these negative responses to emotion and challenge. They are the first step in gaining control of your life and relieving yourself of chronic distress. You know that nothing is working but you don't know what to do differently or what other people do to remain emotionally stable.

Not only are self-soothing skills essential for peace of mind, but for developing healthy and satisfying relationships as well.

Children from dysfunctional families are rarely taught to self-soothe, as their parents don't know how or even that such a thing exists. The children fend for themselves emotionally and develop some of the difficulties described in Part I and Part II. Not only are self-soothing skills essential for peace of mind, but for developing healthy and satisfying relationships as well. When these skills are missing, you react with rage or blame when things are not going your way, often making things worse. You lash out at others to protect yourself from unpleasant feelings or thoughts. If you choose to act out during those times, you're likely to alienate those around you, bringing on more negative emotionality in a vicious circle. Sometimes the rage or pain gets directed inward and you hurt yourself.

If you approach difficult situations in a calm state, you are better able to deal with whatever is happening. You're less likely to make rash decisions or act out in some harmful way. Poor decisions are made when you are in a negative emotional state. A lot of this has to do with your inner language that is revealed in the next Step, *Cognitive-Based Work*. As you improve your inner dialogue, the need to self-soothe may lessen. However, there will always be times when you feel less than ideal. So having these tools in your emotional arsenal is a good thing. Remember, the whole point of the Dysfunction Interrupted program is to feel good!

The Self-Soothing Techniques

With all of this in mind, choose from the following techniques for self-soothing. I recommend that you have at least three so that you don't tire of one of them, making it lose its' effectiveness. Be prepared to engage in one when you begin to feel lousy. It's essential to have a strategy in place rather than winging it with your previously utilized poor strategies or habits. "Failing to plan is planning to fail" becomes a guidepost for you.

Give each of the techniques you choose a little test-run so you know the ones you like ahead of time. By planning ahead, you're taking control of how you will now handle the less than ideal times in your life. Think of it akin to hurricane or earthquake preparedness: you get some water, food, batteries and other essentials. For your emotional world to be successful, you're gathering the emotional equivalents of these for times of distress.

1. **Talk to someone.** We are social creatures and find comfort in each other in difficult times. Try to talk to someone who lifts your spirits so the time is spent productively. Talking to someone who is very negative can leave you feeling worse than when you began. Talk to someone about fun or uplifting topics; don't commiserate about how lousy things are. This is not soothing; it just validates how crappy you feel. If you have a work or volunteer project or anything that interests you, engage in conversation about that. You'll feel better

immediately. (Note: Be careful not to produce burnout in your friends and family. If you feel your needs are excessive or your friends are tiring of your problems, talk to a counselor instead.)

2. **Distract yourself.** Do something that completely absorbs and interests you. This is not the same as denial. This works as it forces you to change gears away from the negative emotionality consuming you in that moment.

- **Organizational tasks** are good, as they allow you to feel some control. This can include cleaning and organizing your house. Organization will be addressed in a later section and some of those tasks fit well here.

- **Humor** is also a good choice. Watch a funny show or read a humorous book if you can't bring yourself to do something active.

- **Do something for someone else.** Research studies repeatedly produce results that indicate that helping someone else lifts a person's spirits and that the result is long lasting. Besides feeling better about yourself, this takes your mind off your immediate problem for the moment and gives you some distance. Just do an immediate act that is reasonable and easily accomplished for now. Later, there will be more on giving of yourself for enrichment purposes. Give a McDonald's meal to a homeless person, offer to return someone's shopping cart, compliment someone, or simply open a door for someone and note his/her response. Think of something that is doable for you today.

- **Engage in your work** if it absorbs you. It will shift your mood and it is productive.

- **Cook something.** This is a creative outlet, and you end up with a great dinner or snack. Give the food away if you don't want it. It doesn't have to be a big batch of fattening brownies; it can be a great salad or vegetable dish. Cooking a food from a different ethnic group can be very stimulating, as it produces novelty as well as distraction. Studies indicate that novelty actually lights up areas in the brain that produce *serotonin*, a brain chemical necessary for good mood.

- **Other novel experiences** that are easy to achieve are taking a different route to work (or wherever you go regularly), using soaps with an out-of-the-ordinary pleasant scent, listening to unfamiliar music, and learning something new. These are simple things. However, through the different senses, you'll be triggering that part of the brain that needs triggering.

- **Engage in your hobby** or start one for this purpose. Painting, carving, needlepoint, etc., give your brain something to do besides ruminate, and you'll be creating something pleasant. Have the necessary items on hand so you can begin the minute you feel poorly. Again, give away what you create if you don't want it yourself. It will be a boost to see someone enjoy your work. Also, admire your own handiwork; it feels good.

3. **Use physical exercise or movement,** as it will exhaust and relax you. Sleep is improved, and you'll be paying attention to your body, as opposed to your agitating thoughts. Mood is immediately improved by the release of *endorphins*. These are brain chemicals that are released, and they help to interrupt the ruminating that takes place when we feel bad. Yoga, Pilates, walking, jogging, any form of exercise is beneficial. Do what you enjoy.

4. Dancing is a good activity to choose as it involves music, which can also shift mood. Just put on your favorite upbeat tunes and start to dance. Do outrageous moves that make you laugh. It shifts the brain from being too reflective. It's time to lighten up.

5. Play games on the computer or a video game. Do a crossword puzzle or Sudoku.

6. Research something on the computer that you know nothing about but that has sparked your interest. Possibilities include travel, science, potential hobbies, and new business ideas.

7. Buy a language program, such as Rosetta Stone or Berlitz and start practicing. Enroll in a class if learning in a group works better for you.

8. Engage in relaxation techniques, such as using progressive muscle relaxation, getting a massage, listening to sound recordings on CD, etc. I will add here that I have tried progressive muscle relaxation many times over the years, and it drives me crazy to lie there and listen to the recordings. I fall asleep or become annoyed and bored to the point that I feel worse than when I started. I prefer yoga or Pilates, as I feel I'm getting more physical benefit and I've included my experience just to let you know these techniques aren't for everyone. Others love relaxation techniques and experience great relief. Remember, what works for someone else, may not work for you—it is why you want different choices.

9. Utilize biofeedback. You will learn how in Step 3.

10. Meditate. Many forms of meditation are out there, as well as products to help you start. As with the relaxation recordings, these can be annoying in the beginning until you develop the skills and start to realize some benefit. I have found that anxious and angry clients who ironically have the most to gain from meditation are the most annoyed by it.

Meditating is not a waste of time. I highly recommend Transcendental Meditation™ (TM) as it is the most widely studied, and the technique has many followers, including many well-known medical professionals as well as creative artists. The literature on TM suggests that you can even feel better within one practice. Multiple studies tout the positive effects it can have on medical conditions, including high blood pressure, migraine headaches and bodily aches and pains. To learn more, visit the website at *TM.org* for information and resources. The site offers instruction but if you Google "TM" along with your city name, you may find ongoing classes within your community. There are many good books written on meditation as well and they are listed in the Appendix at the back of this book.

11. **Get in the car and go for a ride.** This is a smart choice when you have a house full of people and can't get some space to yourself. Just go to a store and look at the merchandise. Go to a bookstore, have a coffee, and research something new. Get away and do something that appeals to you.

12. **Be kind to yourself.** This is not the time to beat yourself up with "woulda coulda shoulda" thoughts or other negative self-talk. Beating yourself up verbally doesn't feel good, and it keeps you grounded in the negative emotionality.

13. **If you truly can't get moving ...** cuddle up with a pet, a favorite blanket, or a stuffed animal and treat yourself like you have the flu for a little while. Watch something uplifting

on TV or an inspiring movie. Think of this as basic comforting. Note: Don't make this your sole manner of self-soothing, as it is the least productive. We're taking you out of the sick and victim mode, not encouraging it.

14. **Use your newly formed self-talk strategies** that you will learn in Step 2, *Cognitive-Based Work*. Test your reactions and thoughts for evidence and reality. Is it even valid to be so upset or have you worked yourself up over nothing? Are you engaging in one of the Dysfunctional Thought Patterns? Do you have the "crystal ball" out? If so, give that thought a tweak to snap yourself out of it.

The immediate benefit of using the self-soothing techniques is to alleviate some of your emotional pain. It allows you then to think more clearly and get yourself back on track without engaging in something that ultimately makes you feel worse. It gives you a tool for life to handle the less than ideal times. Emotionally successful people have a cache of these items that they utilize when times get tough. Remember that your goal is to be emotionally successful.

If you blow your diet or exercise program one day, you can use your self-soothing techniques to get back on track. That's instead of heading to Dunkin' Donuts. If you experience a relationship breakup, ditto. We're all going to feel poorly at one time or another. It's okay to just feel lousy some days. Tell yourself that is what you are doing, feeling lousy, and that you do not need to act upon it. Just be, and it will pass. You're never alone in feeling poorly. We're all connected and in this boat of life together. The motivation to master the self-soothing techniques is that the better you are at it, the quicker you'll be out of distress and not adding to it.

Techniques with self-soothing are now under your belt, and you are on your way to the second Step of your program. Keep your arsenal of self-soothing techniques in mind. As you delve into different parts of your life and attempt to make changes, it may cause some distress. And, as you start to explore your relationships, set boundaries, and employ new life skills, it may feel weird to you and really weird to those around you. Don't be surprised if you upset the proverbial applecart with others in your life; they will act out and even cause you some distress. This is the time to pull out the self-soothing approaches when any type of stress arises.

When memories come back of unpleasant times or childhood events that were negative, self-soothing is what you want to kick in. If you're calm and comfortable with yourself, you will be able to withstand the memories or thoughts as they come back. Then you can compartmentalize them or let them come in and go out again, without having to drink yourself into a stupor, eat yourself into a coma, or run for the Xanax bottle. Remember, they're just thoughts and memories, not live monsters that can literally gobble you up. They're like a Chucky Doll sitting in a chair in the room with you; they are there and they can be distressing. However, they're not going to be allowed to run the show.

Tasks for Step 1: Self-Soothing

Task #1 Try some of the examples given or think of your own self-soothing techniques. Practice them **before** you feel poorly to make sure they are in fact comforting and not annoying to you. Make sure to have the materials needed on hand so you don't have to search for them or go to a store when you need them. List your choices here.

Task #2 Practice this mantra, "I feel like crap but I don't have to act on it. I don't have to do anything right this minute".

Task #3 List here what you might have done in the past to make yourself feel better. Go ahead, all of the dysfunctional behaviors you may have engaged in an attempt to lift your spirits or blot out something bothersome. These are the very things you are now going to stay away from so they need to be named and seen for what they are. These are typically going to be the behaviors we defined as poor coping strategies.

Task #4 List here the times or situations that you know will likely bring about disturbing emotions for you. Can they be eliminated or do they need to be dealt with on an ongoing basis? If ongoing, choose your self soothing techniques and have them ready at the times that you have identified. Maybe you will be able to eliminate the distressful situation down the line.

Cognitive-Based Work

"The thoughts we choose to think are
the tools we use to paint the canvas of
our lives." —LOUISE HAY

Cognitive Psychology and Cognitive Therapy are based on a theory maintaining that how one thinks largely determines how one feels and behaves. If you process information incorrectly, or with some personal bias that has been developed, it will cause emotional difficulty. The focus in Cognitive Therapy is to identify a client's bias, or *schemas,* and follow how it plays a role in his or her day-to-day functioning. This process is the crux of feeling better, and almost all of your other work will tie back into this idea.

Individuals from abusive homes may see the world as full of danger. Depressed individuals may see their lives as something they have no control over. Anxious people who feel vulnerable to death may interpret

> **Understanding and applying cognitive-based skills is the difference between you controlling your mind or allowing your mind to control you!**

every case of indigestion as a heart attack, bringing on panic and more anxiety. It's easy to see how these thinking styles cause distress.

Cognitive Therapy has been found to be the most effective treatment modality currently available. It provides clients more immediate and long-lasting results than other forms of therapy or medication alone. Introduced by Aaron Beck first in the 1960s, there are a plethora of self-help books and programs based in Cognitive Therapy available on the market today. I have listed some excellent ones in the Appendix section. If after completing this book you decide to seek professional assistance locally, look for a psychologist who practices Cognitive Therapy. I cannot stress enough how important cognitive work is in ending emotional dysfunction. Regardless of the type of dysfunction you're experiencing, this is likely to be an important part of the answer. It's rare to make significant life changes without mastering these principles of cognitive-based work. It is the difference between you controlling your mind or allowing your mind to control you!

In this Step, the main points of cognitive work will be examined and the necessary concepts to master will be introduced. Trust me when I say that this is not that difficult, just different. I ask that you not be skeptical. You can Google or search the terms "Cognitive Psychology" or "Cognitive Therapy," and see for yourself the success rates, the history and the range of use. If you have been in therapy, you may already have been introduced to the concept and not known that this was what you were doing!

Cognitive-based work is what's going to set you apart from the unhealthy thinking styles of your family of origin. Chances are your family had a screwy or otherwise unproductive way of thinking, and that is the crux of your problems today. You learned certain patterns of thought or interpretations of the world based on their interpretations. You may also have developed poor thinking habits in relation to your *Limiting Beliefs* which we will discuss a bit later. You will also see how your *Attributional Style* as well as your

Locus of Control will affect your thinking and contribute to what I call *Dysfunctional Thinking Patterns*. I find that clients feel very empowered when they realize that they are in control of how they think, and they actively engage in negating the thoughts handed down from less than great thinkers. That is, in fact, the only thing in life you really have any control over.

For the purposes of interrupting dysfunction, what cognitive work means for you is that you have to start to examine the way you think. The major point for you to grasp throughout Step 2 is that your thinking is directly tied to your emotions. **Your emotions are not random.** If you're feeling poorly, chances are that you're thinking about something upsetting. You cannot feel good when you're in the midst of upsetting thoughts. Likewise, you cannot feel bad when in the midst of optimistic, productive or "good" thoughts. Start thinking about this using the ideas below and apply these concepts in your daily life. That will start you on your way to feeling better. Then you'll see if you can master this yourself or desire professional assistance in the form of psychotherapy or coaching.

The topics that you will learn about that will change your life forever are:

- Your beliefs
- Inner language
- Dysfunctional thoughts
- Poor word usage
- Locus of Control
- Attribution Theory

Examine Your Beliefs

Most of us will find that we harbor some fairly *negative beliefs* or what are called "limiting beliefs." If you are in the "most" category, you approach the world with this set of beliefs in place. The result is that you are less likely to be emotionally or otherwise successful. This is about an actual set of ideas in your brain that govern how you approach the world.

If you believe that you're stupid or unlikeable, this will limit you.

If you believe that you know all there is to know and have nothing to learn, this will also limit you.

If you believe that success is not for everybody (just the lucky people), you won't strive for success as you have already talked yourself out of it.

Think how depressing these beliefs are or how anxiety-producing they are and how poorly that can make you feel. If you replace the belief of "I am stupid" with "I have at least the same average IQ as anybody or I wouldn't be functioning as well as I do," you'll feel better already. No longer are you limited by self proclaimed stupidity!

The first Part of this book looked at a variety of true stories of how families help create beliefs. Did questions surface as you read through them? Questions such as:

Why would anyone want to use the same set of dysfunctional beliefs that a family member used?

How did he or she come to think he/she was stupid, ugly, fat or whatever sorts of things were running amok in his/her minds?

Did a parent, teacher, or some small-minded guidance counselor influence or seed his or her thoughts and beliefs?

This sounds like how I was treated ... spoken to ... raised?

No one is born with the beliefs that they are stupid, ugly, fat, incompetent, etc., and that includes you. Starting today, now, you need to develop your own beliefs and they need to be non-limiting in nature in order for you to function at the best level possible.

The most common themes having to do with negative or limiting core beliefs are: those pertaining to being incompetent, unlovable and unwanted; not good enough to participate in things you would like to participate in; feelings of being defective, broken or damaged in some way; inferior to others or in chronic danger of some sort. With these beliefs in place, you can see where everything in life that you would like is going to be beyond your grasp as you believe you cannot or should not reach for it. When they are present, it is hard to achieve and be successful, experience the love and acceptance of others and find a sense of belonging in the community. You will see in the next Step how these thoughts affect your body as well. So right now, sit for a moment and write down some of your beliefs that may need rearranging.

Most *core beliefs* (basic beliefs) stem from your past experiences, and they are extremely powerful in dictating how you now live your life. They can be extremely limiting if you don't challenge them. You have to sort through and eliminate the unhealthy beliefs that were inherited or learned. In turn, you create your own set of empowering beliefs, new beliefs. The majority of your actions are a result of your beliefs.

Your Inner Language

Your thoughts are made up of your words. Your choices in words have a huge impact on your life experiences and emotions. Are you using your parents' words or are you using your words?

Words are your primary tool for translation. Therefore, the words you use to describe or label your experiences dictate the sensations or emotions produced in your body (measurable with biofeedback, a key part of interrupting dysfunction and described in the next Step).

An equation used in therapy to help clients understand this process is:

$$T=PR$$

or

Thought = Physiological Response

What this means is that every thought you have carries with it a physiological response or a shift in your body processes. Think about it. When you think about negative things or have upsetting thoughts, you have different bodily sensations than when you're thinking about positive things or have uplifting thoughts. These bodily responses don't come out of the blue. Panic attacks, anxiety and depression don't just come out of nowhere with the exceptions of the medical conditions previously described. They're directly related to your thoughts and interpretations. Below are a few examples of the emotions stemming from different sorts of thoughts.

> **Scary thought** = Panic and anxiety = Heart racing, hot or cold flashes, etc.

> **Sad thought** = Sadness, Drain of energy = Fatigue

> **Perception of another's wrongdoing** = Anger = Adrenaline and cortisol surge

I'm not saying that bad or scary things don't happen, or that when they do, you should be immune to them. How you interpret things on an ongoing basis, every day of your life, is what causes distress if you're using a negative schema or interpretation.

If you have been taught that the world is scary, you look and interpret almost everything as a potential danger. If you have been raised by the "Sad Sorts" identified in Part I, you may see everything as hopeless and out of your control. Remember the link between learned helplessness and depression. If learned helplessness is your schema, you're going to be depressed. The overall thoughts of depressed individuals exhibit negative interpretations of the past, of the future and of their abilities.

If you were raised by the "Here Today and Gone Tomorrows," you may see every slight by someone as a sign that they're ready to leave. You, in fact, will probably be watching for that very slight every day of your life. If your boyfriend or girlfriend is distracted … Boom! You interpret this as he or she is ready to hit the road.

Scary indeed! These may not be thoughts you would have developed if you had been raised in a different or even healthier family. So you cannot hang on to them defensively, like you are losing part of yourself or some critical part of your personality if you change them. With the steps you are taking, you are ridding yourself of them for the betterment of your own life. You are taking control of your thoughts and the resulting bodily accompaniments.

Twelve Dysfunctional Thought Patterns

There are typically 12 dysfunctional thought patterns or misperceptions that individuals engage in that cause misery. They're described here to allow you to judge which ones you may use on a regular basis. Typically, you have four or even five favorites!

We're all guilty of using them at some time or another–it doesn't mean there is anything wrong with you. They're just ways of thinking that you have learned that create unhappiness. Being able to recognize when you are engaging in them, which one or ones you gravitate to, will help free you from the negative emotions that result. It also enables you to develop more constructive thought patterns and enjoy the resulting positive emotions. Your body likes this better too.

As you read through these, keep in mind the equation, **T = PR,** *Thought = Physiological Response*, and test for yourself how these thought patterns make your body feel.

Someone doesn't smile at you and you decide that they are angry with you for some reason. In order to help you with this concept, I have created a chart for keeping track of your daily thought patterns. Go to *PsychSkills.com*, opt into the "Dysfunctional Thought Patterns" free download and print it off for daily use. This whole concept is there in just a few pages for easy tracking.

1. **Things are one way or the other; there is no in-between or middle ground.** You see things in absolute categories. "I blew my diet with that ice cream cone; I may as well eat everything else I want also." "All people of different religions are scary." This type of thinking has a rigid feeling, is often irrational and it tends to stymie creativity in the individual. It is also often a thinking pattern that doesn't allow for negotiation in a relationship or life in general, thereby limiting the potential for happiness. If the absolute belief is negative in nature it will promote anger, depression and other negative emotions.

2. **Extension:** One negative event carries over to all such events. "I failed that test. I will always fail tests. I am no good at tests." "My partner left me; no one will ever love me."

3. **Black Filter:** You notice and dwell on the negative aspects of things. You have had dinner in a nice restaurant, the food

was great, the service was good; however what you think about is that your cab was 15 minutes late. This will bother you to the point that the rest of the evening almost doesn't matter.

4. **Not Recognizing the Good:** You ignore the positive aspects of yourself or your contributions or you don't recognize them for what they are. It's hard for these individuals to accept compliments. You may say to them that they did a great job and their response is typically, "Anyone could have done it. It was nothing." By not acknowledging the positive, you cheat yourself out of the accompanying warm and fuzzy feelings. You also can't build upon your strengths if you don't recognize and utilize them.

5. **Mind-Reading:** You interact with someone (even briefly) and decide what it is he/she is thinking with absolutely no evidence. Someone smiles at you, and you interpret it as a look of pity meaning you're about to lose your job. Someone doesn't smile at you, and you decide that they are angry with you for some reason. It then eats away at you all day, when the reality is that the person was just distracted that morning.

6. **Predicting the Future:** You get out your mental "crystal ball" and predict that things are going to have a bad ending. You feel convinced that your prediction is already an established fact. It's like you see an entire horror movie played out before your eyes but you're in reality just thinking it up. For example, you hear that it's going to snow a bit the day you have to go to the dentist. Your mind conjures up a ten-car pile-up resulting in death and dismemberment. Your bodily response is one of panic. You get the idea.

7. **Catastrophizing:** You think in terms of the absolute worst and may blow things all out of proportion based on the actual event. This is when everything is treated as if it were catastrophic when it's really not. Spilling something is not the end of the world, nor is the end of a relationship. Painful maybe, but not a catastrophe.

8. **Problem Shrinking or Denial:** On the flip side, you may go through life minimizing problems in an unrealistic way. You could say something like, "He only drinks when he's stressed" instead of saying, "He's an alcoholic." When you're not realistic, you are not able to deal with what is in front of you. Your emotions are then confused and leave you feeling disoriented.

9. **Distorted Emotional Response:** You allow your emotions in the moment to dictate your overall thoughts. "I feel stupid right now; I must be stupid." You can see based on the **T = PR** equation how this is going to leave you feeling. If you miss a golf shot you may tell yourself, "I am a loser, I am a terrible golfer." The obvious better response would be, "I missed that golf shot, and I need to practice."

10. **Personalized Expectations or Judging:** This is where you view the world based on your own value system and expectations of others. Words like "should" come into play here. "Should" is by nature a very judgmental term and suggests something or somebody is lacking in what "should be." This can lead to anger and disappointment. You might prefer something be a certain way, but that doesn't necessarily mean it "should" be that way. This is also applicable to ourselves and pertains to developing reasonable expectations for our own behavior and outcomes. "I should always be perfect"

is not a reasonable expectation and will result in disappointment for the individual who has incorporated this into his or her life beliefs.

11. **Mental Name Calling:** Mentally beating yourself up is just as hurtful as if someone else called you a name to your face. When thoughts like "I am a fatso"... "I am a loser" or "Okay stupid ..." filter through your brain, they get you nowhere fast. The result is a feeling of sadness and zero self-worth.

12. **Finger Pointing:** Blaming others for your problems can be an easy way to think of things but is rarely correct. The flip side of this is blaming yourself for things that you are not to blame for. If you are stuck in a bad relationship, it is easy to point the finger at your partner but you really have to look at yourself and wonder why you are there to begin with. Abused individuals often incorrectly blame themselves for the latest argument or fight as this is what the abuser has repeatedly told them.

Before explaining how to dispute these scary patterns, I have a few other concepts I would like you to grasp. Then you'll put all of it to work at once.

Adopting a New Vocabulary

Let's go a step further. It's not enough to conquer the dysfunctional thinking patterns. You now have to replace them with better and more productive thoughts and words. In his many books and seminars, Tony Robbins discusses *Transformational Vocabulary*. He states:

> Simply by changing your habitual vocabulary—the words you consistently use to describe the emotions of your life—you can instantaneously change how you think, how you feel, and how you live.

If you consistently use angry or negative words or words packed with too much emotion when the situation doesn't warrant it, you'll upset yourself needlessly. It's amazing to think that somehow your vocabulary can direct your emotional life! What a concept! But it's true. Think about it, the words of great leaders and people you admire have awed and motivated millions of people for centuries. The words you choose help you to communicate with others. You know or can see the effects of your words on others if you have chosen unwisely. These same word choices affect also how you communicate with yourself and how you end up feeling.

Your own words direct you on a day-to-day basis. You have the power to use these words to strengthen yourself and transform your existence from one of misery to one of power, happiness and strength. Amazing!

How do you neutralize these upsetting thoughts you have with some of your word choices? A critical question that has an answer. By this: *replace the words you have chosen.*

Look at the following examples below, and keep in mind the **T = PR** (*Thought* = *Physiological Response*). Which column allows you to feel better and enjoy a better life experience? It doesn't invalidate that you aren't feeling the best possible. However, it keeps you in the game by allowing you to move forward and not get stuck in negative ruminations.

Bad Word Choice	Good Word Choice
I am depressed.	I have had a little setback.
I am anxious.	I am a bit concerned.
I am really ticked off.	I am annoyed.
I am overwhelmed.	I am busy.

In Tony Robbins' book *Awaken the Giant Within,* he gives many examples. The chapter on transformational language is unsurpassed in explaining this concept to the point of mastery for all readers. Not only do I highly recommend this book, if you have the opportunity to attend one of his live seminars, I suggest you do so.

Locus of Control

Nothing feels worse or more depressing than thinking you have no control over your life or destiny. The essence of who you are cannot be carried out and fully realized until you take control of yourself and your life.

But, what if you have reached adulthood believing that everything that happens to you is beyond your control? Or that all the good things happen due to luck or chance, not that you have brought them about by your own behavior or effort? If you think that way, you are likely to just sit back and

> **Your efforts are what matter in life building; your decisions and your actions have everything to do with your outcomes.**

wait for some other stroke of luck to hit. The results limit you, as you are not reaching for your goals or building a life of your choosing.

> An *Internal Locus of Control* is where you believe that your outcomes are contingent on what you do to make them happen. They are a product of your own decisions and efforts. *External Locus of Control* is defined as the belief that your outcomes are contingent on events outside of your control; they just happen due to fate, luck or chance.

External locus of control is not ideal in life building. And all of this is created in your head, not in reality. Yes, you may experience some fortunate circumstances. Yes, you may experience some unfortunate experiences. However, they cannot be utilized as a means to build an entire thought process.

Your efforts are what matter in life building; your decisions and your actions have everything to do with your outcomes. Even if a hurricane knocks your house down, your efforts at rebuilding or moving are what count in how you will come through the event. If you sit back and wait for the next hurricane, you're not going to feel fulfilled or satisfied with your life. If you get up, and get on with things the best you can, then later you will tell yourself, "Wow, I didn't have much to work with but I really came through that pretty well." The difference now in your power and how you will address other life circumstances will be huge.

Developing a Healthy Approach

It's actually healthy to have a bit of both thinking styles in your repertoire. If you fail and then tell yourself that you're totally a loser, when perhaps there were some extenuating circumstances, then you're likely not to try again. On the other hand, you'll be more likely to believe you will have success in the future if you're able to say, "I did my best but it was hard due to a lack of knowledge," or if you know that some specific circumstance, like the weather, was a factor in the failure.

So, where are you right now? Do you believe that your outcomes so far in life have been a product of your own abilities, actions and ideas? Or have they been a set of random circumstances brought on by fate? Take a minute and examine where you believe yourself to be. Be very honest here with yourself if you are examining less than ideal behaviors. You also need to be kind to yourself if you have been doing nothing out of a belief that you're not able. The whole point of this exercise is to see where you are, how you got there, and then make the necessary tweaks to get into a more ideal frame of reference. So remember, the goal here is to develop a more Internal Locus of Control that allows you to feel more in control of yourself and your life. This brings with it such an amount of peace, you won't believe it.

When something bad happens, you'll be able to examine it to see where maybe you could have done better or where you made a mistake. Everyone makes mistakes. If something was taking place in your environment, it is okay to place some responsibility on that as well. For example,

- It was raining and you couldn't get good footing in the race. (Consider different shoes for better traction next time.)

- You didn't do well on your proposal because the kids were noisy and you couldn't concentrate. (Then make sure that you find a quiet place to work next time.)

If there's something to be learned from the experience, learn it and move on. Don't beat yourself up; it's not the end of the world. Maybe you made a huge mistake, and it cost you a relationship, savings account, even a job. You still have to move on and learn from it. If you lost your job because you showed up drunk, it's your fault. It's not due to the fact that your friends kept you up partying all night. It was your responsibility to get to work sober. You made a choice.

When something good happens, you'll be able to take credit for it. That person is dating you because he or she likes you, not because there's no one else available. You got the job because you're qualified and obviously did well in the interview; it's not because the HR person was sick that day and wanted to get the process over with. You have a nice home because you worked hard to earn the money for it; it's not because the mortgage company gave you the loan in error.

Taking credit is fine. You're not bragging or being arrogant, it's just the way it is. If someone or something else contributed to your success, give them credit as well; there's enough to go around. But know that you created whatever the event was.

Once you master these principles, it simplifies life tremendously. You've attained the springboards to work from that are now clear and you know where to focus. You'll learn to remove the obstacles in your thinking that keep you from living to your full potential. You no longer choose to continue to live in a cycle of defeatist behaviors.

Time is wasted waiting for luck or chance if you are externally oriented. If you know you have some ability and believe you do, you can act now. Once this concept is clear to you and you have examined and tweaked your *Locus of Control*, multiple doors will open that were closed before. Regardless of how your orientation came to be, it can now be right, and you don't have to spend a lot of time on it. It becomes an everyday component of who you are.

Locus of Control is not a new psychological principle; it has been around for years. You're not being asked to disregard or lose an important part of yourself or to change your personality. You're simply adding a skill base that will allow you to be happier, more productive, and more in control of your life.

Attribution Theory

One last concept in the cognitive area that I would like to introduce you to is *Attribution Theory*. Much research in Social Psychology has stemmed from this idea, and it has produced interesting and consistent results on how thinking affects emotions. Studies even show that as early as playground experiences, you are interpreting and attributing behaviors and causes of behaviors to others. It is likely that you began to make these attributions based on some of your parents' thinking styles modeled during your early development. If you observe someone who is behaving in a certain way, whether the behavior is correct or not, you draw conclusions based on what you see.

This is similar in concept to the mind-reading thinking pattern. You watch people, interpret the events, and these interpretations then make you feel a certain way—good or bad. There are two types of attributions that you make:

1. *Internal,* where you decide that a person is behaving in a certain way because of some inherent quality they have; or

2. *External,* where you decide they are behaving a certain way due to a current situation or outside circumstance.

Your emotions, responses and reactions are all now going to be based on the attribution you have made.

Consider these examples:

A person steps on your foot while standing in line.

Internal attributions: The person is careless and stupid and stepped on my foot. Or, the person didn't like me and stepped on my foot on purpose.

External attribution: The person was bumped into and lost his/her balance and stepped on my foot. It happens.

As you can see, when you utilize an internal attribution, you can get fired up pretty easily at whatever is going on. This is especially true if you have extended to them a negative attribution. The external attribution leaves you thinking, "Okay, the guy stepped on my foot, no big deal." How you respond to this person, however, is a big deal if you shove him back or yell at him because you decided to go with the negative internal attribution of him having done something bad to you on purpose.

A co-worker doesn't speak to you one morning as he usually does.

Internal attributions: He is rude; he is ignoring me on purpose. He thinks he is better than me.

External attributions: Maybe something bad has happened to him this morning, or maybe he's on medication for something and he is feeling whacked out.

Your emotions, bodily responses and direct responses to the person are going to be affected by whichever thought you chose to go with. If you have chosen the first or the Internal Attribution, you will be angry and feel that you have been treated poorly. You may also then make decisions throughout the day that affect how you work with him. But what if you choose the latter thought, that of something being wrong in his life in that moment? You will instead feel empathy or concern and will treat him accordingly. You will not feel anger. Your ability to thwart angry responses can be this simple in concept.

These are choices you will learn to make with practice. This is not to say that everyone's intentions are benign and that you won't encounter a few jerks along the way that are just that—jerks. With jerks, you just have to limit your encounters and choose your thoughts to say something to yourself, such as, "I'm glad I am not a jerk like that person. I feel badly for him that he has no friends because he chooses to be such a jerk."

You get the idea. You come out ahead with these thoughts because you have not put your body into an uproar over something you can't control—like the fact that someone is a jerk.

What Makes You Angry?

Things people do and say, things that happen that feel unjust—from the cable company not coming to your house within the scheduled time frame, to the Internet connection not working to someone saying a stupid remark can trigger anger. Sometimes it's an ordinary event, while other times, it could be something more serious. But as stated before, anger is a very unhealthy emotion. And it is your words and your thoughts that actually make you angry. The event is the event—it is how you translate it into your own reality. What you attribute the problem to is key.

The cable company is not infuriating, the delay is a nuisance. The person who cut you off on the highway is in a big hurry, not out to beat you to where you're going. And maybe he is getting sick or headed to an important meeting. *Big deal, let him go.* Sometimes it's hard to let it go if you're accustomed to this internal thinking style. You'll be able to really see how your body responds to angry thoughts in the next Step that focuses on biofeedback.

One of my clients was challenged every time he got in a car. Commuting to work and back gave him an arena to act upon his anger against the whole highway. Swearing, weaving in and out, honking his horn, he was in his element, and of course the conditions never disappointed him. There was always a slow person in the fast lane. There was always someone talking on their phone … someone who didn't speed up to make the light … someone who didn't take off the minute the light turned green.

You name it—all the personal traffic situations that are normal occurrences became a venting highway for him. He actually looked forward to his commutes, as it gave him roughly two hours a day to become very angry. I taught him about self-talk and dysfunctional thoughts in our sessions. We examined reasons people do the things the way they do, such as driving too slow. Up until that point, he felt it was a personal affront and a product of someone's stupidity. When I asked him how his aged mother drove, he looked a little abashed and said, "Slowly." When we discussed how people on medication might drive or people with limited abilities, it became clear to him that the world was not out to annoy him. Drivers were just doing their thing, the way they needed to.

Learning to argue against your pessimistic thoughts in an effective manner relieves depression, and it is as *effective* if not more so than anti-depressant medications.

From that point, it became easier for him to be in traffic. He learned to utilize the time with tapes and audio entertainment. Later he reported feeling much better when not engaging in two hours of anger daily. He said it was actually now hard for him to become angry, even when he wanted to react that way. If someone drove slowly, he would picture his mother driving and another person honking and swearing at her. He said that whenever something started to irritate him now, he could hear my voice asking him which screwy thought he was engaging in, and it ruined it for him! He would instead start laughing that I spoiled this for him. Self-talk can turn around your thinking, and therefore your emotions. Laughing is far more soothing than being angry!

Pulling It Together

You're now aware of all the Dysfunctional Thought Patterns, the Locus of Control issues, the importance of word choice, and Attribution Theory—all the biggies in keeping you stuck in unhappy and dysfunctional thought patterns. How do you turn these patterns around?

Learning to dispute your dysfunctional thoughts is the key. This does not mean sugarcoating things or living in denial of some sort, but using your mind logically and rationally to examine what you are thinking and why it is causing you distress. Studies show that learning to argue against your pessimistic thoughts in an effective manner relieves depression, and it is *as effective if not more so* than anti-depressant medications. There is also less chance of relapse.

By using a cognitive model to dispute your negative thoughts and distortions, you can alter your reactions. Simply put, you are going to question these thoughts and do some investigative work into your mind based on the answers to these critical four questions:

1 What just happened?

2 What was my first thought?

3 How do I feel right now?

4 Is it reality?

A few examples of how this works from an easy one to more complex are:

Example 1

Using the scenario from above, you are standing in line and someone steps on your foot.

1 Event = *Someone steps on your foot.*

2 My first thought = *This guy did this on purpose because he wanted to get to the front of the line; people are selfish and think only of themselves. (Mind-Reading and Extension are going on here for distortions.) You have also projected an internal attribution to the event (purposeful behavior, rather than external circumstances).*

3 How do I feel right now? *I feel angry; I want to shove the guy into next year. I also feel angry in general that people are such selfish jerks. I am disappointed in the human race and feel negative toward them in general. I will stand in line and fume, and in fact may relive this moment over and over all evening to the detriment of my good time. I will ruminate on what a jerk he is all night. I will also consume my mind thinking of all the things I should have said to him, causing me further anguish. I will be in such a negative state that no one will be able to stand* *to be around me all evening. The toxic feelings that have developed in my body feel terrible.*

4 Is it reality? *I really don't know that he did it on purpose. I have no evidence to suggest this. In fact the person in front of him may have bumped into him causing him to lose his balance. He may be dizzy or lightheaded from medication that he takes. He may have just lost his balance for no particular reason.*

I feel better and the anger is dissipating. I really don't care anymore about the guy, and I will give it no more thought. I will go on with my evening and have a great time. My negative or pessimistic thoughts have been neutralized, calming the T = PR process and allowing me to go on in a constructive manner. I have thought it through logically and rationally, and I believe and accept my new thoughts. I didn't just try to change my thoughts by saying something like, "Oh, Mr. Nice Man stepped on my toe. What a great guy!"

To take it a step further, you are also operating from an *internal locus of control* where you decided to take an event and handle it yourself in a positive manner and not let it control you. You were presented with an adversity and decided to change the way you felt because you did not like your current feelings. You did not just wait for something else good to happen to counter or replace the negative feelings.

Example 2

1 Event = *My significant other seemed distracted at dinner. He/she did not show much interest in our conversation or in me in general.*

2 My first thought = *He/she must be tired of the relationship and is getting ready to end it. I will be financially strapped without his/her income and will have to get an extra job. I will also have to buy new furniture. I knew I was unlovable when* *the last relationship that I had ended; I should never have gotten into a new relationship. He/she is probably having an affair. (Anxious attachment, Mind-Reading, Extension, Predicting the Future, Mental Name Calling, Judging)*

3 How do I feel right now? *I feel scared for my future. I now can't eat my dinner. I am thinking about all the bad things about this person so I can soften the blow when he/she ultimately ends this. I will have thought of enough stuff to convince myself it doesn't matter because he/she isn't that great anyway. I am lonely because I am now detaching from him/her to prevent more pain. I am feeling very defensive, and I may try to pick a fight in order to end the waiting and just get it over with. I am angry that he/she is cheating on me. I am going to pick a fight for sure now.*

4 Is it reality? *I have zero evidence that he/she is thinking of ending the relationship. In fact, I have more evidence to the contrary. When we spoke today, everything seemed okay. Everything in general seems to be okay; he/she hasn't voiced major concerns about the relationship and we have been talking long-range plans. I know he/she is experiencing work/family/ health/financial concerns right now that may have come to the forefront this afternoon. I will just ask, "What's the matter?" and take it from there. I need to quiet these thoughts and enjoy his/her company and dinner right now. If the behavior continues, we will need to work it out, or maybe this isn't the right person for me. I must be somewhat loveable as I have enjoyed other relationships.*

I now feel better, and I was able to focus on dinner and the moment at hand. I quelled my panicky thoughts, which allowed my body to get back to normal (T = PR). I relaxed, became more open and conversational, and attempted to get the person to discuss his/her day. If nothing else, I am not going to let this screw up my evening out. Also, my attitude of examining this relationship from the point of view of whether it meets my needs puts me in a position of control over myself and my destiny (internal locus of control).

Example 3

1 Event = *I did very poorly on a test today.*

2 My first thought = *I am stupid. Now I will not enter graduate school and be caught up in a menial job the rest of my life. (Mental Name Calling, Predicting the Future, Poor Word Choice)*

3 How do I feel right now? *I feel sad, depressed and much self-hatred for being stupid. I am not even going to bother to try again. I think I will go eat/drink/use whatever other poor coping strategy I can think of. I feel as though my future is now very limited.*

4 Is it reality? *I guess I am really not stupid. I passed all the requirements to get into college to begin with. I have no evidence of actual low intelligence. I did well on the SATs and that takes some level of ability. What really happened was that I allowed myself to get distracted from my studying by my social life, and I wasn't as prepared as usual. I can change this by not allowing that to happen again. One bad score is not going to result in being removed from school or prevent me from getting into graduate school. It's not ideal that this happened, and I am not going to let it happen again, as repeated failures will result in negative consequences for my future.*

I feel better, more in control, and not as pessimistic about my future. My mood is lifted again, and I have the motivation back to try harder and control my circumstances.

The concepts of Cognitive Psychology and Cognitive Therapy will take you to a new level of functioning. Cognitive Therapy as used in practice and the treatment of individuals with emotional difficulties running the gamut from depression to attention problems has been shown to be the most effective. It has the longest lasting results and is more effective than medication alone. Why bother with anything else?

When mastered, the concepts of examining and changing your Underlying Beliefs, paying attention to your Inner Language, eliminating Dysfunctional Thought Patterns, tweaking your Locus of Control if necessary and evaluating the Attributions you make to the world around you are already enough to see you on your way to feeling better. Most likely, you are able to see where a lot of your unhappiness may have stemmed from these learned thought processes. Remember, you were not born with these. You now have the opportunity to change them.

Tasks for Step 2: Cognitive-Based Work

Task #1 Your task is to now go back over this material and decide which Dysfunctional Thought Patterns you may be engaging in and how often. Download the information PDF on Dysfunctional Thought Patterns that includes the tracking chart from the home page of *PsychSkills.com*. For one week, keep track of which ones you favor and utilize regularly, as they may be the culprits in keeping you feeling poorly. Two days' worth is enough to allow you to see what you are doing if you find yourself chronically unhappy. It will take a bit of reflection initially to determine which ones you are doing. However, after that, it will come easily, and you'll be able to identify immediately which distortion you have used. Do not skip this task; it is a critical step in starting to feel better immediately.

Task #2 Think about your vocabulary. Which emotionally laden words do you use regularly to describe your life experience? Do you use words like terrible, horrible, depressed or infuriating? Remember, these set the tone for your moods. Go through your words and find replacements.

What words do you use that are infused with emotion? Start to practice this daily. Chances are that you'll find your emotionally laden words in the content of your Dysfunctional Thought Patterns. An example of this would be: "I know I will have a horrible time adjusting to my new job." This thought is going to result in distress to you. You are not only *Predicting the Future* but your forecast involves disaster (horrible time). Better phrases or thoughts would be: "I don't like change that well but I'll do fine" or "My new job may be a challenge but I can learn new things." Write down the words you are trying to replace so that it's clear to you which words need to be discarded.

Task #3 Pertaining to interpersonal matters, think through the last upsetting exchange or thought you've had regarding someone's behavior. Using Attribution Theory, is there another way to explain his/her behavior? Does it have more to do with how you're thinking than the actual event? Do you have evidence that the way you have interpreted the event is correct? If the event is still bothering you, is there a way to clarify the facts? If not, can you just let it go?

Task #4 Now pull it all together and think of some of the larger scenarios that are common for you or that have occurred recently and are fresh in your mind. Using the 4 Question model, work them through like in the examples. Identify the Dysfunctional Thought Patterns and Locus of Control or Attributions that you are using as well. Let's see if you can make yourself feel better immediately about some of the things going on in your life right now. Pick a really distressing scenario if it is possible and get that knocked out.

Biofeedback

"Destiny is not a matter of chance,
it is a matter of choice;
it is not a thing to be waited for,
it is a thing to be achieved."

—WINSTON CHURCHILL

B iofeedback is a technique that has been utilized by the field
of psychology as well as medicine for decades. It's a medium
of treatment that has been well researched and determined to have
many positive effects. In biofeedback, individuals are basically
trained to improve their health and well-being by learning to read
signals from their own bodies. It teaches the user to become aware
of various physiological processes that occur under conditions such
as stress. Instruments are attached to the body in a non-invasive
manner to provide information on the activities going on in the
bodily systems. The individual is then able to learn to manipulate
the bodily reactions for better results.

**Using biofeedback can be likened
to any bodily measurement, such
as taking a temperature or reading
blood work.**

For example, you can be trained to
raise the temperature in your hands.
What you are actually learning is to
relax the vessels to allow blood back through. Using biofeedback
can be likened to any bodily measurement, such as taking a

temperature or reading blood work. Biofeedback provides useful information about how you are doing and enables you to use that information to improve your condition. Within this Step and for the purpose of interrupting dysfunction, you will utilize it to assist in improving your mental health. It's most effective combined with relaxation and positive self-talk.

To delve into this a bit deeper, the definition of biofeedback that has been approved and adopted by the Association for Applied Psychophysiology and Biofeedback (AAPB) and the International Society for Neurofeedback and Research (ISNR) is as follows:

> *Biofeedback is a process that enables an individual to learn how to change physiological activity for the purposes of improving health and performance. Precise instruments measure physiological activity, such as brainwaves, heart function, breathing, muscle activity, and skin temperature. These instruments rapidly and accurately 'feedback' information to the user. The presentation of this information— often in conjunction with changes in thinking, emotions and behavior—supports desired physiological changes. Over time, these changes can endure without continued use of an instrument.*

The AAPB and ISNR monitor the field of biofeedback, and serve as resources for information, practitioners, equipment and training programs. You can go to a practitioner's office for biofeedback or purchase one of the devices designed for home use. If you choose a practitioner in your area, make sure he/she is trained and has certification.

Types of Biofeedback

Practitioners may utilize one or more types of biofeedback. Their equipment may range from a simple computer program that measures one of the following, or they may have a complex system that can provide you with feedback in all of the following areas at once.

Temperature Biofeedback: When you're anxious, your skin temperature is lowered as blood is moving toward muscles and internal organs for "protection" purposes. Learning to control skin temperature has been shown to help with the cessation of migraine headaches, as it directs blood flow back to the extremities. This is one measurement that is typically included in the home devices.

Electromyogram (EMG): The EMG measures muscle tension by reading signals from sensors placed over the muscles to be monitored. For example, neck and shoulder, as well as facial muscles, are typically contracted in an anxious individual, and the person learns to relax these muscles using the "feedback."

Galvanic Skin Response (GSR): This type is also known as *Electrodermal Response (EDR)*. It measures electrical conductance in the skin, which is actually associated with the processes of the sweat glands. The more stressed or anxious you are, the more sweat gland activity is going on. The device gives you a measurement that you are then taught to manipulate by will.

Electroencephalogram (EEG): The EEG measures and provides feedback regarding brain wave activity. This is the least precise and most complicated form of biofeedback, and chances are you will not experience it unless you visit a practitioner with all the bells and whistles.

Heart Rate Variability (HRV): This measurement is based on the idea that your emotional state affects your heart rate by measuring the subtle beat-to-beat shifts in heart rate. HRV is thought to be affected by emotions, thoughts and environmental stressors. This heart rhythm pattern indicates how your nervous system is being affected by stress.

Sympathetic nervous system arousal is indicated in the distressed individual with a visual display of a jagged heart rhythm. When shifting to a more positive state, the parasympathetic system kicks in and produces pattern changes to a smooth rhythmic pattern. Both the sympathetic division and the parasympathetic division are regulated by the autonomic nervous system. This type of measurement can be done at home with the emWave device, which is described under Biofeedback Games and Home Devices in this chapter.

Heart coherence reduces nervous system chaos.

It's believed that positive emotions induce better thinking, which is why you are more creative or find insight into problems when you are not stressed. This technique is utilized in peak performance training and gets excellent reviews from consumers.

The benefits of HRV coherence are improved cardiovascular and cognitive performance, better decision-making, reduced pain sensitivity and improved reaction times among others. The Institute of HeartMath has done research in this area for many years, and it refers to "coherence" as the optimal physiological state. The goal then is to achieve this state called coherence, defined by the HeartMath organization as a *state of synchronization between your heart, brain and autonomic nervous system, which has been proven to have mental, emotional, physical and even spiritual benefits.* Heart coherence reduces nervous system chaos.

Self-Monitoring with Biofeedback

I love the empowerment biofeedback gives clients as they begin to see themselves in control of their emotions through breathing, self-talk and self-monitoring. This is particularly good for those with panic and anxiety, who suffer dizziness, lightheadedness and the fear of passing out. It's utilized for treating anxiety and stress, high blood pressure, attention problems, and a variety of physical ailments that are either believed to be caused by or exacerbated by stress. It is also widely used by trainers and coaches to improve performance in executives, performers and professional athletes.

Let's say you experience anxiety to a very unpleasant level. When the body is anxious, breathing, temperature and other bodily responses are off normal or off what is ideal. Stressful events and thoughts produce strong feelings or emotions that bring with them many physical responses. These responses are generally controlled by the sympathetic nervous system, which is the system in charge of emergencies.

The typical response of the body is for the gastrointestinal system to slow down, you begin to sweat or feel hot, your pupils dilate, and blood vessels contract in the extremities while those in the muscles and brain dilate to increase oxygen. Your heart may beat faster, and your blood pressure rises. If the event is specific and situational, you will return to normal functioning when the danger has passed. If the event is ongoing, such as fears, chronic stress or continuing abuse, your body may live in that state, and it may feel normal to you, even though you know at some level that you're uncomfortable.

In Step 2 on Cognitive Based Work, I discussed how your thoughts dictate your physiological responses. Biofeedback is the tool that gives you the visual on this phenomenon, especially if you are a visual learner and you like "proof" that it is working. Learning

Theory also indicates that the more modalities in which you are taught something, the more it sinks in.

Here's an example of how this works. You're hooked up to the machine and thinking your normal scary or stressful thoughts. You see the colors or lights or sounds the machine is registering, and they indicate a high level of distress. You now use your cognitive techniques from Step 2 to tone this down a bit and take control. So if your thought is, "I will never be happy or feel normal," chances are the machine is telling you that your body isn't happy with this thought. You then replace it with "I'm working toward happiness, and I am a good person with a lot to contribute."

Remember how good the positive thoughts feel versus the negative ones? You are now repeating that process here as a visual with bodily involvement. The goal also is to pay attention to your breathing and purposefully start to breathe deeper and more calmly. The breathing exercise I recommend (because it's easy and works!) is to breathe in deeply through the nose and then out slowly through the mouth. You can think it through in your mind this way,

In through the nose, out through the mouth.

And the pacing for an effective deep breath is about the same time it takes to think those words. *This becomes your mantra whenever you feel yourself becoming panicked or experiencing unpleasant anxiety or stress.*

The processes work together, and you should see the biofeedback program start to register a more ideal "score" or indication of progress over time with use. As a demonstration, I then encourage clients to upset themselves again by saying something like, "I am worthless" or "I cannot ever go outside because the world is a dangerous place" and then watch the resulting feedback from the program. Because of the negativity, it will indicate now that they are headed back to the "poor score zone."

Next, their wording is changed to something positive or more realistic. Not surprising, the feedback moves back toward normal. Amazingly, those few words impact the body and the biofeedback measurement reflects it. The client can really see how their own thoughts control this process and so will you.

This is a great visual on how catastrophizing and some of the other Dysfunctional Thought Patterns from our cognitive section affect our bodies. Even if you haven't mastered the language and thoughts part yet, you can benefit by watching the machine go up and down— just based on your ability to force yourself to breathe properly.

You feel better immediately when you take control of your breathing and physical responses.

Breathing itself is an important concept, rarely thought about and often taken for granted. One reason you get lightheaded is not because you're going crazy but because you aren't getting the right amount of oxygen. This is similar to hiking to Pikes Peak in Colorado or some other high altitude; there isn't sufficient oxygen in the air for some and it's easy to become woozy. The biofeedback machine helps you learn proper breathing, and it visually demonstrates what the ideal breathing rhythm is for you. Until you pay attention to how you breathe (and few do), you don't realize that you're even breathing improperly. You'll feel better immediately when you take control of your breathing and physical responses. Just understanding this process brings relief in knowing you are not going crazy. Reminding yourself of this when you are out lessens the likelihood that you will be overcome with wooziness.

Biofeedback Games & Home Devices

The companies who have designed the biofeedback programs have made them into fun games and special effects experiences also. There is a meditation learning option in the *Wild Divine* package that builds a rock wall or takes your rocks away based on your temperature and breathing. Doors open, beautiful peaceful scenes are presented and they are really quite creative and fun. I find that clients like such effects, as they take the emphasis off dysfunction and place it on learning optimal functioning. They are teaching you control and how to relax and be more effective.

The *Wild Divine* programs also offer guided meditation and training.

The portable devices, such as *emWave 2* by HeartMath and *Stress Eraser* (available at Amazon), allow you to carry them with you and utilize the techniques "on the go." Many clients have difficulties with anxiety in public, while driving, when traveling or at work, and these devices allow usage while in the midst of the real life stressor. This is very effective and both devices are easily learned.

The bonus for you is that you learn that you can be in control of things you probably thought you couldn't control. You see it happening in real time, right in front of you. A calm mind is a calm body. Calmness is good. You'll enjoy better focus and productivity, better relationships and better health. I have had success with many clients over time with this process, and the common denominator with their feedback was the relief they reported feeling. They now knew that they could control the panic, anxiety and terror that had been keeping them from enjoying their lives.

The ultimate goal then is when you are out shopping, getting ready to fly, or do a presentation, that you can realize your fear or nervousness has to do with how you are thinking about the situation. By changing your thoughts and paying attention to your breathing, you can go ahead and do it. One day, it automatically becomes, "I feel upset so I must be thinking something screwy and therefore my body is not in sync. I will become aware of my thoughts, adjust them, breathe properly and off I go." This will only take a few seconds once it becomes second nature to you. Right now, it may seem impossible.

Some of the most popular biofeedback programs and devices are:

EmWave2: Designed by the Institute of HeartMath, this is a small handheld device, easily carried in the pocket or purse. It runs on a lithium battery and measures your heart rate variability. You can clip a monitor to your earlobe or place your finger on the designated area on the machine. A pattern of lights helps you to establish coherence by breathing and shifting yourself to a more positive emotional state. HeartMath offers the following background on their website: "Stress creates incoherence in our heart rhythms. However, when we are in a state of high heart coherence, the nervous system, heart, hormonal and immune systems are working efficiently and we feel good emotionally."

A calm mind is a calm body.

The emWave2 Personal Stress Reliever helps you reduce your emotional stress by displaying your level of heart rhythm coherence in real time ($199, *HeartMath.com*). It's also available for Desktop Mac and PC. I have found the customer service at HeartMath to be excellent whenever I have had questions or ordered products.

StressEraser is also a small handheld device that runs on AAA batteries. You place your finger into a slot, and it will begin to display a wave-like pattern of your breathing rhythms. A graph on the front of the device gives you real-time measurement of your breathing, and it trains you to reduce stress by activating your parasympathetic nervous system. You are given "points" for successful breathing and relaxation, and the device indicates goals for what is considered an effective session. There's also a program for nighttime use called the **Relaxing Nights Program,** a 15-minute routine to be used before bedtime that is supposed to have carry-over effects of stress reduction.

Wild Divine Relaxing Rhythms Guided Training Program: In association with Dr. Deepak Chopra, Dr. Dean Ornish and Dr. Andrew Weil, this program runs on your home PC and trains you in breathing and meditation exercises using the finger sensors provided. You practice the exercises and receive real-time feedback. Soothing visuals are offered onscreen or you can watch your graph display. There are great special effects and games with the exercises. Cost varies depending on product package purchased. (*Wilddivine.com*)

Note on working with a biofeedback practitioner

Before leaving Step 3, it's important to add a few comments on working with anyone who claims to be an expert in biofeedback. If you decide to practice with a professional, check with the Association for Applied Psychophysiology and Biofeedback (AAPB) and the International Society for Neurofeedback and Research for a recommendation of practitioners who are in your area. State laws governing biofeedback practitioners vary. Ask if your insurance will cover the practice, some do not. Also make sure that you're comfortable with the biofeedback practitioner because you will not do well if you aren't or if you do not feel safe.

Tasks for Step 3: Biofeedback

Task #1 Find out if there is a biofeedback practitioner in your area and whether or not your insurance covers the cost of the appointment. If so, it's well worth trying it. Just go for a couple of visits to get the idea and see how it benefits you to have this information. Then invest in a home or personal device for continued use if you feel you're receiving benefits from the practice. If it's not possible to attend an appointment, invest in one of the devices for home use and use it as recommended in the accompanying manual.

The makers of the home devices offer good information, and follow-up questions for usage are answered quite well. They also all come with a money back guarantee. If you don't care for the first one you try, don't be discouraged. Just try another.

Give yourself a good month to practice and receive benefit. You did not become anxious and distressed overnight. You are used to being anxious and distressed so now you have to get used to being calmer and in control. It is not unusual to resist change as change represents newness and newness can also be scary.

Task #2 Once you have determined how you will practice biofeedback, begin to do it regularly with your home device. Do it in particular when you're upset. That way you can see your physiological response to your thoughts and practice your cognitive work from Step 2 while doing this. The device will give you a visual on how this process all works together. Then practice while you're calm or engaged in your self-soothing to see the response of your body.

Step 4

Advanced Thinking Skills

"Of all the creatures on earth, only human beings can change their patterns. Man alone is the architect of his destiny ... Human beings, by changing the inner attitudes of their minds, can change the outer aspects of their lives."

—WILLIAM JAMES

Within Step 4, you will take the basic cognitive work that you completed in Step 2 and ramp it up a notch. It's a long chapter with many key concepts so hang in there. You've learned how to neutralize Dysfunctional Thought Patterns and begin to break these negative thought patterns with better thoughts. You've also learned how your thoughts affect your body, as well as how your language and the very words you use contribute to this process. With that information and adding *Advanced Thinking Skills* to it, you will advance to the next level of functioning. That will be the level where you focus on *what you want,* not what you don't want, where you leave misery in the dirt, where you achieve your goals and feel excited and passionate about life. *Good-bye dysfunction!*

Advanced thinking means thinking in correct ways, eliminating poor thinking habits, and also eliminating poor personal habits. You don't often put much emphasis on your personality, accepting that how you are is just the way you are. However, this isn't necessarily true. What you learned in Part I is that much of what you are has been developed through learned habits. Your thinking has influenced your personality and the way that you interact with others. The habits and ways that you direct your life are also a product of your thinking styles.

The habits and ways that you direct your life are also a product of your thinking styles.

If you have developed some less than ideal traits, then now is a good time to eradicate them in order to move forward and experience life more fully. If your parents had awkward or even no social skills, what is the likelihood of you developing any? If you have been too shy or withdrawn to form satisfying relationships due to poor self-esteem, then this is the time to fix that as well. If you perform poorly at work due to misguided thoughts, it's time to alter old patterns and habits.

You will now learn the Advanced Thinking Skills set associated with success in all areas of life. Step 4 will include the topics of Purpose Definition, Strengths Awareness, Focus, Laws of Attraction, Right Questions, Goal-Setting, and Personality Check. These critical concepts must be mastered in order to bring about a positive and creative lifestyle, one that is free from dysfunction. This skill set is really quite easy to learn and will appear almost moronically simple in concept.

The feelings that will arise will astound you in their pleasantness as well as the excitement for life that accompanies them. You'll feel better than you ever have. And it all takes place right upstairs in your mind. I placed the Advanced Thinking Skills chapter early on in the program so that you become excited about your life. Also, it's been placed here so that you learn to think and focus your thoughts properly, in order to derive the most benefit from the entire program.

Powerful Concepts

The Advanced Thinking Skills are not new concepts by any means, and I am not the inventor of them. For each concept I have included resources or the names of individuals whose original ideas these are so that you may read further if interested. I have chosen to bring them together in one program because I believe they all are important, valid, and have a place in psychology and the treatment of individuals with differing emotional issues. They have been around forever but haven't made their way into mainstream psychology as we know it. Outside of serious mental illness, they mean the difference between major relapses in your mental health or ongoing emotional success.

These skills are the premise of many motivational and success programs and the messages are critical for all, not just those seeking financial wealth. The author Napoleon Hill did a great job in defining a lot of these concepts in two of his books: *Think and Grow Rich* and *Napoleon Hill's Keys to Success: The 17 Principles of Personal Achievement*. Rhonda Byrne's *The Secret* was published in 2006 and is based on the **Law of Attraction.** It puts forth that **positive thinking** combined with intense focus can create life-changing results such as increased happiness, health and wealth. Her book complements Hill's principles and reads very quickly. (*The Secret* was also made into a movie.) These concepts have been utilized by some of the greatest minds and talents of all time. Why not learn to think like successful people, as opposed to those with dysfunction?

> **Why not learn to think like successful people, as opposed to those with dysfunction?**

People spend mega-millions of dollars every year attending self-help and motivational seminars to learn these exact same skills. I believe that they have a place in psychology in the actual "cure" for many emotional ailments and should be part of anyone's psychotherapeutic treatment. This is not just a skill set for individuals who are already fine and just want a boost to more success. You'll see how they are the very skills that will actually take a person with some dysfunctional traits to an entirely different level quickly, without years of costly therapy.

In traditional therapy, most clients' treatment ends after the majority of their symptoms have left through cognitive or other therapeutic work or after having been medicated. The diagnostic criteria necessary for their insurance to continue to pay for anything other than medication checks is no longer met. Hopefully, a client has a bit better skill base but often not one yet of excellence. At some point, he or she usually winds up floundering and falls back into therapy or suffering through another bout of whatever he or she had to begin with. Small percentages turn to life coaches, mentors or others who can guide them to feeling good. Yet there are others who don't realize what they need and feel lost. No one has advised them that advanced thinking can help, and it does help tremendously.

You can see very successful people in your world or in the media, and when interviewed, they often list roughly the same habits and thinking patterns. They were not born with these skills; they learned them somewhere along the way. Maybe it was their family, maybe not. Some people simply observe and read about those who are successful and emulate their actions.

My definition of success is happiness in life and relationships, as well as career. It's really not enough just to get through your day. You need to get through your day with excitement and in the best form you can. As humans, it's the only way that we achieve real happiness and fulfillment. Rather than this being considered a luxury, I feel it is necessary for most people who suffer from any of the difficulties previously discussed. Obviously these skills were overlooked or not taught for many reading this book, yet they are the very skills that are essential for your overall happiness.

When you're functioning at your optimal level, there's no room for maladaptive patterns such as attention problems, anger issues, anxiety or any of the others to interfere with your happiness. You'll be building an emotional wall that keeps out these negative predators. When one penetrates the wall, it is dealt with swiftly and sent on its way.

Have a Purpose

The first concept of the Advanced Thinking Skills to understand and embrace is that you have to have a *purpose in life*. Without this, you are aimlessly going through your days and are not focused on what you want out of life. Think of it as having no real plan in place. When your attention isn't focused and you're not moving forward, all the emotional ills that you can experience start to really take hold.

What else is the brain to do? It's working constantly, and if you haven't given it a direction or a purpose, it will find one of its own. If it feels lost with no purpose, it does its version of "acting out"— by making you feel anxious and sad and all over the place. Having a *sense of purpose* develops self-reliance, personal initiative, imagination, enthusiasm, self-discipline and concentrated effort. *These feel great!* Having a well-defined purpose also interferes with depression, anger problems, anxiety, attention problems and more. It keeps you on track when you start to feel lost.

So what is *your purpose?* To explore this, clear your mind of all your problems right now and just focus on this exercise. You may determine that your purpose is career-based, such as, "I want to create a new product," or you may have one that states, "I want the next level promotion in my current job." You may just want a different job altogether. You may want to change things for the better for an underprivileged group or wish to help make conditions better for wildlife or the environment. Your purpose may be to raise your children to be the best individuals that they can be. It could be to become an artist.

Everyone has something that he or she believes in and feels passionate about; you have to determine yours. Start now by making a list of passions or interests of yours. Just brainstorm a bunch of them; never mind how outlandish they seem at the moment. They won't seem so outlandish later. Steer clear of purposes like "I will no longer be depressed," as then you are still focused on depression. That might not make sense right now, but it will soon.

I want you to focus on something other than mental health. Clearly define that purpose. For example, my purpose right now is to use my education and years of experience in psychology to help as many individuals as I can. When I began my purpose, I didn't worry immediately about how it was going to happen. I just decided that that was my purpose.

Once you accomplish your purpose, you'll either build on it or find another purpose to focus on. This is not a onetime exercise to make you feel better; this is a way of life. Think of it as having something to live for.

- If you are anxious, you could now be worrying about whether you have chosen the "right" purpose. Stop—don't worry about that, as it is fine along the way to tweak the purpose, or allow that purpose to guide you to another purpose. This is a starting point and there is no right or wrong.

- If you are depressed, you may be thinking that there is no purpose for you or life in general; please remember that those thoughts are the products of pessimism, not of who you are.

- If you are angry, you might think that there's no way to reach your purpose because something will get in the way or block you.

Remember that these thoughts are products of the distorted thinking that you eradicated in Step 2. Don't worry—it's hard to eliminate this thinking immediately when you have thought this way your entire life. So this is a gentle reminder to put those thoughts away and allow yourself the pleasure of finishing the program.

Signature Strengths

When deciding on a purpose for life, it helps to know what Positive Psychology calls your *Signature Strengths*. These are a major concept in this field. They help you make the very best of who you are in a way that is not only pleasant to you, but also compels you to continue to move in a forward direction.

Why not define yourself by who you are by personality rather than by what disorder you suffer from? The theory does not deny that everyone has weaknesses—but, weaknesses do not have to dominate a life.

Don't ignore your weaknesses. They may at times be serious enough to hold you back, create disruption in your life and relationships, or even affect your health. But the weaknesses are also not what are going to move you forward. Weaknesses can be likened to a leak. Stretch your imagination—think of yourself as a sailboat with a small leak ... a leak is your weakness. If you concentrated solely on the "leak," you ignore a vital strength—the sails. They have the ability to move you in almost any direction, offsetting the minor leak. If your entire focus is on the leak, you will not make gains that the sails, your strengths, can deliver.

I have placed Signature Strengths in the Advanced Thinking skill set as traditional psychology and sometimes even mainstream society tend to have a focus on the weaknesses. As a result, an inordinate amount of time is spent defining, diagnosing, prescribing, and otherwise dwelling on weaknesses as opposed to strengths. As you will see in later sections of this Step, that is rather backwards when seeking overall well-being. Psychologists Seligman, Rashid and Parks revealed in *Scientific Research* in 2006 that therapy that uses a strengths-based focus outperforms "therapy as usual" and "therapy plus antidepressant medication" comparison groups.

> **Signature Strengths are those that bring about a feeling of excitement while engaging them as well as a feeling that time is "flying by."**

We all have Signature Strengths. Finding ways to utilize them and incorporate them into your daily living is one of the keys to a sense of well-being and satisfaction. Signature Strengths are those that bring about a feeling of excitement while engaging them as well as a feeling that time is "flying by." Individuals are thought to feel a sense of truly being themselves in the moment while utilizing these strengths as well as feeling energized rather than drained while using them. Enthusiasm and a desire to continue with more projects that also use the strengths are a frequently reported result of harnessing these Signature Strengths.

You may be wondering, "How do I go about finding my strengths?" First, think about times that you were successful at something or performed at something very well. What traits or natural talents were you using? Maybe your strength was that it took great perseverance to accomplish whatever it was; maybe it required courage or leadership. Other strengths involve cognitive areas such as curiosity and creativity.

It is likely that there are certain behaviors others will notice in you while you are engaging in or discussing things that incorporate your strength. You will become animated, and you may use more hand gestures, more fluent speech, better posture and a more direct gaze. Can you think of times that you feel this has described you?

It is not always easy to identify your strengths as you may not have given it much thought in the past. Your problems may have felt more pressing, and you may have believed that they required more attention. You may have taken your strengths for granted and not realized that they too needed to be fully developed. There is an entire language or group of words that concerns strengths that you may not be familiar with. For whatever reason, if your strengths have not been identified and developed, it is time to do so now.

The Authentic Happiness website, *AuthenticHappiness.com*, is based in Positive Psychology and offers a personal strengths survey called the VIA Survey of Character Strengths. The survey takes roughly 15 minutes (all you need to do is go to the site and register—it's free), and it provides your results immediately. You can then print them out to keep on hand. More than a million people from two hundred nations have taken the survey—you have plenty of company. Your highest ranked five strengths may be your "signature strengths."

After identifying your top five, apply the signature strength criteria. Notice how they make you feel while you are engaged in using them. Sometimes you have a strength that you've developed out of necessity, and it doesn't produce good feelings. For example, you may have learned how to manage other people as a requirement of your job and over the years become quite proficient at it, but you may hate every moment of it. So this is not a natural or signature strength. When you are engaged, most likely time moves very slowly and painstakingly.

When you have determined what you believe your signature strengths to be, you will then begin to think about and focus on ways to incorporate them into your life at every opportunity. Your purpose will also incorporate these strengths. Look around the *AuthenticHappiness.com* website while you are on it; there are many other surveys and questionnaires to explore. There are also opportunities to participate in research, blogs about others focused on strengths, and so on. It is a great website and filled with very useful and positive information—tools that are all free.

Focusing on What You Want

Now that you have defined a purpose and identified your signature strengths, your next skill to learn and practice is *focus*. You won't attain your purpose if you don't focus on it. Focus also keeps you moving forward, allowing you to reach whatever goals you have. If you aren't focused on what you want, you won't get it. It's rare that something just happens and you receive what you want without having given it some pretty serious attention. Your focus is related to your purpose in that you're thinking constantly about achieving it. This constant thought is your focus. You're focused on getting what you want and taking the necessary steps to get you there.

If you aren't focused on what you want, you won't get it.

It's very important in this concept to understand that your focus is to be on what you *do want,* not what you don't want. If your focus is on what you don't want, your mind is still consumed with what you don't want, and this is not exciting or productive.

Let's say you have a less than desirable mate right now that you know probably has to go. Yet you like having a mate and don't want to be alone forever. Rather than think about all the bad things about this person that are making you unhappy, start instead to focus on what you do want. Picture and focus on what would be a great partner–what qualities, what would he or she look like, and how would this person act toward you?

Get excited about this new partner, and quit thinking about the old one or the bad parts of the old relationship. Maybe the old one needs a little direction in what you do want, as opposed to what you don't want, which you're probably sharing regularly with him or her—either vocally or in your own behavior. Maybe he's an abusive jerk and really does need to go.

Now, consider how these thoughts are making you feel. When you're thinking about being mistreated, it makes you feel bad, and that is what we're moving away from. When you get excited about being treated wonderfully, you feel good, hopeful and excited. This is the difference in focus.

Another example would be a work situation. Let's say you hate your job and want a new one. Recently you've been sitting around and thinking about what a lousy job it is, how lousy the pay is, and how your boss mistreats you. As you saw in Step 2, *Cognitive-Based Work*, this will keep you feeling terrible. Instead, how about turning your focus to your new purpose, and thinking about your ideal job and the qualities that will make it a dream come true? Then you'd get excited and look forward to that. If you remain focused, you'll begin to look for a new job, and think about that process as opposed to ruminating about this current job. This task or learned skill of switching focus in order to keep moving toward happiness is one that you can practice every day, and it's critical to your well-being.

What Are You Attracting?

This concept of the Law of Attraction is quite well described in Rhonda Byrne's cleverly titled book, *The Secret*. She brought together many successful, famous and inspirational individuals to share their thoughts on what they call "The Secret." The "Secret" itself is that:

> *Everything that's coming into your life, you are attracting into your life. And it's attracted to you by virtue of the images you're holding in your mind.*

If you haven't already read it, consider it a must-read. I cannot do it full justice here within this limited section. It is available in both book and audio format as well as a movie.

To fully grasp the concepts, it's essential to read the book. Essential elements of the core to it are: People who drew wealth into their lives have used "the Secret." They think only thoughts of abundance and wealth, and they don't allow any contradictory thoughts to take root in their minds.

The same goes for happiness and contentment. Thoughts of happiness and contentment bring further thoughts of happiness and contentment.

If you think predominantly about depression, you'll draw more depression. If you think only of how anxious you are and of what you're afraid of, you'll only draw more fear. If I was summing this up, it would be this:

**You manifest what you want; what you want to be.
Not someone else. You.**

When first reading about this concept, some feel that they're being blamed for causing their difficulties or unfortunate circumstances. This is not what they're saying. What they're saying is partially about what was discussed earlier on focus: What you're thinking about is determining how you're feeling. If you're always thinking about depression, you'll draw more depression, as that is the predominant idea in your brain. Your brain does what you're telling it to do, and it focuses on what you're telling it to focus on.

The words and thoughts associated with depression are depressing! I'm not saying you do it on purpose; it's typically something you don't even understand you're doing and that is why you're learning about it here. That is also why this new approach is called Advanced Thinking Skills.

For example, if you're depressed, you may have daily thoughts along the line of:

- "I am so depressed."
- "Where is my depression medication?"
- "When is my next doctor's appointment?"
- "I am so depressed, I can't get going."
- "I can't take another day of being depressed."
- "Everything is bugging me because I am so depressed."

See what I mean? These are not thoughts you cook up to keep yourself depressed; they're simply the thoughts you're having because you haven't been taught the value or reasons to have the other sort of thoughts. I really want to emphasize this as I know these ideas can bring about defensiveness as clients feel they are being blamed for their emotional difficulties. Don't be defensive, you are not being blamed. Your brain just hasn't been trained to focus differently. I think you can see, however, that the previous thoughts all have their focus surrounding depression.

Instead of the above thoughts, picture having a day when your thoughts are along the lines of:

- "How will I work toward my purpose today?"
- "What fun thing is on my schedule for after work?"
- "How much can I fit in this day that will take me toward my purpose?"
- "Will I meet a new partner today?"
- "What great thing can I make for supper?"

You get the idea; no thought is on being depressed. So in order to feel good, we don't want to be focused on the topics of poor mental health.

Two other important ideas from *The Secret* include:

1. Your life can change if you consciously choose what you think about.

2. It's impossible to feel bad if you're having good thoughts.

Think about how powerful these two lines are. I have utilized these ideas in my life many times before recommending them to you, and they really work!

Asking the Right Questions

Another skill in advanced and successful thinking is learning to *ask the right questions* of your brain. Again, a seemingly basic concept, and not new, this idea has been around forever. However, it hasn't been incorporated into mainstream psychology. When you ask the right questions, you get better and more productive answers than when you ask the wrong ones.

Consider the following examples.

Poor Questions

Why am I so depressed?

Why did I have to be born into that family?

Why is the world so scary?

Better Questions

What can I do to be happy?

What makes me happy?

What is my next adventure?

What do I have to do to become successful?

What are my strengths?

How can I use my strengths today?

These better questions all push you to action, and the actions are the opposite of sitting around feeling miserable. Think of some questions you typically ask yourself. Are they poor questions or good questions? Use your cognitive work and better language skills to reword and rework them. Your questions need to be part of your focus and should have the ability to move you toward your purpose. Don't ask useless questions whose answers are irrelevant to your success. Your brain will give you the answers you need; just ask your brain the right stuff.

Goal Setting

Setting goals is a large part of being effective and being happy. It's part of the skill base that keeps you on track. When you don't have goals, you float aimlessly and life passes you by. You may have had a goal like "get through college," but then no others to follow it up. Or "I want to get married," but once it was achieved, you didn't create a new goal. When you're in a state of pointlessness with no purpose, you're bound to be unhappy and weird emotions creep into your brain. The uncomplicated and simple reason why you may feel you have underachieved could be because you have failed to set goals.

A goal may be about getting organized or achieving a certain level of proficiency at a hobby or sport. Whatever it is, you can set the goal and then attain it. Goals keep you moving. It's easy to see how, if you have limiting beliefs, you won't set great or exciting goals. You will already think that you can't achieve them. When you allow yourself to be set up this way, you end up paralyzed—it's why negative beliefs need to be deleted. You feel good when you achieve things. Life is going to happen anyway and time is going to move ahead no matter what you do. You might as well design and utilize your life the way you want it. So set up the steps you'll need to take to achieve your goals. Set goals in each area of your life. When you meet those goals, set the next group and move toward those. And when you haven't met a goal, examine what's hindering you; you might find the answer somewhere in your thinking. Goal setting is a seemingly simple step but it makes all the difference in your outcomes. Goals give you focus and an action plan in working toward your purpose.

Goals keep you moving.

The most effective individuals always have goals in place and are working toward them. They have something planned that excites them and keeps them wanting to get up in the morning. Your job is to find that which *excites* you. Something to look forward to that keeps you going. It buffers you from feeling hopeless when something bad happens. Chances are something bad will happen at some point; it's in the numbers. People die, people get ill, fires and earthquakes happen–all of it bad. If you're buffered

You feel good when you achieve things.

enough with self-confidence, positive activities, good friends and thoughts of what's good and will be good again, you're less likely to get sucked down in the mire of whatever bad thing has happened and not be able to find your way out again.

Below is an example of goals you could set in order to benefit the most from this program. It's not enough just to read the list. You have to work it by setting the goals and checking them off as you master the concepts. I also

> **Goals give you focus and an action plan in working toward your purpose.**

find that when you set a goal, it boosts your chances of success if you place a time frame with it and the exact way it is to be carried out. I personally have daily, weekly, monthly, and six month goals in place as well as long term such as one and five year goals.

Goals for Successful Completion of the *Dysfunction Interrupted* Program

1. Read the program and do the tasks at the end of each step.

- Finish reading by Friday.
- Review more difficult parts again by Sunday.

2. Find a method of self-soothing that works for you. Use it as necessary. Find a backup in case the first one is not doable for some reason when you need it.

- Try things that are of interest from the list of potential self-soothing activities listed in this book.
- Go to the store and buy materials if needed.
- Have these in place by Monday.

3. Find a biofeedback machine and learn to use it.

- Research websites and products recommended.
- Place order by Tuesday.

4. Utilize one of the three recommended diet/healthy eating plans. Buy a book or sign up online. Set up a goal, such as a weight loss amount, a fitness challenge, or even a health goal such as to lower your cholesterol.

> • Goal is to run a 5K in September.
>
> • Check with doctor to see if I am okay to do this.
>
> • Find a trainer or training program for home use.
>
> • Follow training program.

5. Utilize Step 6, *Enrichment,* to add positive and rewarding experiences to your life. List three things you can add and add them.

> • Go to bookstore and do the exercise from Step 6.
>
> • Find hobby and start researching or chatting online about it by Wednesday.

You get the idea.

Personality Check

Here is the last concept in this part of the program, and you may initially bristle at the idea. Working on building your self-esteem by making sure your personality is in order becomes a crucial key to interrupting dysfunction.

If you were raised in a dysfunctional home, it is common to learn or develop personality traits that were adaptive in the home— traits that you may have needed to adapt to or even survive in the household. These same traits may not be so adaptive in the broad spectrum of the world with your peers. You may even be lacking in basic knowledge of etiquette, which is easily obtained in any bookstore. There can be possible relationship ramifications if your personality does not include some of these positive features that have already been identified in previous Steps. Having this information under your belt gives you the confidence to feel comfortable in whatever social circle or activity you may find yourself.

If you see qualities listed here that you haven't thought about developing, it doesn't mean you're a loser. It just means that you haven't given any thought to them.

We grow up thinking that this is who we are; we're not even aware that certain qualities require polish or development. Rarely do we pay attention to the fact that these traits can affect our mental health. Yet, they are related to it.

> **Your personality traits have everything to do with how you feel, how you look at life, and how others perceive you.**

If you don't have the social skills to blend with a desired group, or if you're not sure how to be in the world, how can you be successful? Many business people will take great care to learn the customs and manners of countries they're approaching for business relationships; meanwhile, they will cut into a line, talk over others, lie to people, or be otherwise rude to their fellow citizens. Your personality traits have everything to do with how you feel, how you look at life, and how others perceive you (and if they decide that they want to be around you or not). It has everything to do with who your friends are and the types of people you attract. The question surfaces: are you attracting the type of friends you desire? If not, it's time to look into your personality mirror.

There are those individuals who reject the idea of personality development or accepting social norms on the basis they feel it takes away from their individualism to be like everyone else. I disagree wholeheartedly with this concept and have never met a happy client who thought like this. No one is asking that you lose your sense of self or become one of the crowd. The place to distinguish yourself from others is in your interests, your career, your intellectual and charitable pursuits, any of the number of things you choose to do that makes you unique. Your fashion sense and hairstyle, the type of car you choose to drive, all those are places where it is fine to stand out.

When it comes to basic manners and personality traits that allow you to move freely and interact well with others, the less experimenting you do, the better. These things have already been thought out and for the most part accepted—you do not need to reevaluate them. Every species has behaviors that are accepted and relevant to the well-being of the group. If a giraffe were to start eating like an elephant, the giraffe community would wonder what is going on. If he continued to behave strangely, he would be considered "sick" or "odd" by group members and they may move away from him out of the fear that he might somehow bring danger to them. A normal response in the animal kingdom would include distancing themselves.

All groups have what are called **norms.** If you adhere to the norms, you are more likely to be accepted by those around you. Incidentally, I also found those clients who initially eschewed these ideas but then adopted them were very pleased with their results. Most want to have friends and belong to a group. I bet you are no different.

Self-improvement gurus as well as motivational and success speakers have long touted the benefits of good personality traits, and they have identified the ones felt to be crucial in our personal success. Napoleon Hill's book, *Napoleon Hill's Keys to Success: The 17 Principles of Personal Achievement* is an excellent resource on this topic and on self-improvement in general. I believe skills of personality that promote success translate over to the individual attempting to defeat emotional ills, as well as to those striving for great wealth or other goals. This personal skill base is just as important to this clientele if not more so as they may be struggling with finding a sense of belonging in a community of their choosing, with work advancement, or with simply getting along with others and feeling comfortable enough to venture out into the world to find themselves. The Advanced Thinking Skills require you to take stock and see where you are in terms of these traits. You can always stand improvement. Why not try to have a great personality?

Key Components in Personality Development

Personality takes a variety of shapes and forms. Some of the major characteristics include:

Be Positive. This doesn't mean you are a "Pollyanna," which is the first piece of resistance I typically hear from a client when I mention this trait. It means you stay in a positive frame of reference when dealing with others. It allows you to present yourself with an openness that attracts others to you. As identified in Step 2, *Cognitive-Based Work*, being positive influences your language and bodily responses as well. It is a win-win situation for you. It allows you to be open to problem solving as everyone does encounter problems. It influences your entire being and appearance to others. The opposite of this, negativity, turns others away.

Be Flexible. Rigidity of thinking limits you, and it can bring with it much unhappiness. If you are unable to "go with the flow" a bit, you will experience anxiety and distress. If plans change and things don't go as you think they **should,** it doesn't benefit you to freak out or lose your temper. Whatever it is will still be happening, and you may as well get through it with some decorum and with your blood pressure intact.

Make Up Your Mind. Much research has been done into decision making, and the results are repeatedly the same. Successful people reach decisions definitely and quickly. Successful people change their mind and decisions slowly if at all, whereas studies indicate that people who are unable to make quick decisions change their mind often and quickly. Practice making decisions quickly—not irresponsibly. But once you have all the information needed, pull the trigger.

Practice Courtesy and Tact. Learn to recognize and respect the feelings of others. Be careful of what you say and how you say it. Sometimes it's better to say nothing at all! Do not monopolize conversations or talk about unpleasant things, including medical details from your last illness or surgery. Open doors for others, don't cut into lines; simply put, practice great manners at all times. There are many etiquette books available; I have listed some in the Appendix section.

Be Aware of How You Speak to Others. Speech is the medium of communication to the world. Your tone of voice can convey many things to the listener as can the choice of words that you use. Tones that sound whiny, very anxious or bossy are likely to elicit a negative response from the person on the other end of that communication. If you use slang or poor grammar or offensive metaphors, you are also likely to put others' off. The same goes for cursing.

Get a recorder or use your microphone on your computer and listen to yourself talk. Say things as you normally would in the course of a day communicating with peers, colleagues, family members and strangers. Do you sound positive? Do you sound like a shrew? Is your tone demanding or timid? How many times do you say "um" or "like"? Listen carefully and decide how you would interpret your personality if you were on the receiving end of that speech. Would you want to talk to you?

Smile. Just do it. Smiling is one of the most important things you can do to make yourself have a pleasant personality. Other people sense smiling even on the phone and respond more positively to you. Smiling has been studied in evolutionary terms having to do with facial expressions, and it appears that smiles let potential enemies know that no harm was meant or that the "cavemen" were friendly and cooperative and not wishing to fight. Other species, such as apes, also exhibit what appear to be smiles when attempting to display cooperation. Try smiling when you're angry; the action itself is calming.

Be Aware of Your Facial Expressions and Gestures. What's going on with your face? Are you prone to frowns or turn your mouth downward as the norm? Do you look suspicious or wary? Just as you listened to your speech, look at your face and see if your facial expressions are those that someone would be attracted to. Do you look open and friendly, or do you have an expression that says, "Get away from me"? Before you even speak, people see your face and attempt to read what it is saying. Make sure it is saying something positive. Practice in the mirror until it is comfortable. This is very important, and not just for everyday life or with work. If you are looking for a mate, you want to attract someone with the positive qualities that you are learning. If you look angry, you may attract an angry partner.

One summer, I heard a speaker whose topic was *Making Sure You Don't Have Resting BIT@#* Face (RBF). What a title! It was a great eye opener for making sure your face is pleasant when you think others might not be noticing. There are facial muscles that will pull downward if you are not careful and will make you appear unpleasant or even annoyed. Her solution was to practice a mini smile as a natural face using only the smallest amount of muscle engagement possible so that it feels natural and resting. If it tires your face or you have to pay too much attention to it you are using too much muscle. Try it until it feels natural and you can maintain it. Save the RBF for when you are really alone! Better yet, don't use it.

Another aspect of this is to pay attention to your movements. Are you picking at your hands or nails while talking? Looking elsewhere? When initially attempting to create videos for my website,

I noticed that I was making what looked like a weird motion with my mouth repeatedly. It appeared on camera to be a facial tick involving my entire lower jaw. What it actually turned out to be was me trying to make sure there was no lipstick on my teeth! In an attempt to look okay, I was making a circus out of my face. That lesson was quickly learned! What I realized was that I probably do this in real life as well and need to eliminate that unsmooth move.

Respect Others. Be tolerant of other people's beliefs and ideas. If you don't agree with their beliefs, ignore it, or if it affects you or your rights in some way, then disagree in an appropriate manner. If negative racial and/or sexist beliefs have been part of your upbringing, then it is time to leave those in the past and move on. Being open and tolerant toward others opens your world even further.

Watch How Others Are Responding to Your Comments. If you see the eyes of your audience glazing over, you are boring them to death. Keep your messages direct and short. If you are asked to speak publicly, find out your time allotment and stick to it. People resent being held over when it is time to go or to eat or whatever they are waiting for. Likewise, do not monopolize any conversation that you find yourself part of. Do not go into all the ungodly details of your medical issues, and although your grandkids are interesting to you, a very brief synopsis of their accomplishments is plenty. Ask questions about others; do not limit the conversation to being about you. People love to talk about themselves, and they will remember those who listen to them.

Give Others Your Undivided Attention. The ability to listen to others is an achievement in and of itself, and it actually makes you more attractive to others. If you give someone the idea that you're not interested in them, they will find someone else to talk to or do business with. Glancing around, taking phone calls, texting or gazing at your iPhone or any other device is rude, and you will insult those with whom you are interacting.

Be Interesting. Find some interests that you can discuss, and try to keep up a bit with what's going on in the world. A few tidbits of knowledge can help you carry the conversation in an awkward social situation.

Whew! This may have been a difficult Step for you. There were many new concepts introduced that you may never have considered as contributing to your not feeling or performing your best. You may have experienced rejection or failure in your past or been floundering about, wondering what to do.

> **Advanced thinking means thinking in correct ways, eliminating poor thinking habits, and also eliminating poor personal habits.**

The value in defining a purpose, *your purpose*; focusing on it; attracting to yourself only the things that you choose and that make you feel good or are productive; and discovering the strengths that you possess that you will utilize to gain the most satisfaction from your life is a lot to put on your plate. Along with that is asking yourself the right questions to get the best answers, goal setting, and finally, looking at personality traits. You may be asking yourself what these topics have to do with your mental health. The answer is **everything!**

I brought these ideas together here as I believe them to be imperative to your overall well-being, particularly if you have experienced a dysfunctional upbringing. The lack of knowledge of these concepts may be what is standing in the way of your happiness and life satisfaction.

There's one final thing to do before exiting this Step and moving to the next. Take the time to complete the following tasks and see how you feel with the ideas all in place. Not only are they for individuals who are already feeling fine and want to experience more success, I believe they are the very things that instill hope and optimism, feeding the human spirit within all of us.

Think about how your power has increased if you master only the second Step on cognitive behavior and this one on skills needed for advanced thinking. Already, you have become a person with different and more productive thinking patterns. That power is what helps you to overcome depression, anxiety, anger problems and more.

Tasks for Advanced Thinking Skills

Task #1. Write down your chosen life purpose from the "Have a Purpose" section of Step 4. Don't worry right now about how you will reach it; just decide on one purpose. You can add or change purposes later.

Task #2. Add some snap to your day. Place a rubber band around your wrist or ankle. When you find yourself focused on something undesirable, give yourself a snap. This interrupts the rumination pattern in your brain, and it brings you back to your new ways of thinking. You'll know immediately when you are focused on something undesirable as you'll start to feel poorly. Use this time to reframe the thought and look and focus forward, not backward. After a few weeks, this will become more automatic as you'll like your results and how you're feeling. You're going to get very good at focusing properly because it feels good.

Task #3. If you didn't already take the strengths survey on *Authentic Happiness.com*, please do so now. Print the results out to keep, and study them to see which you believe to be your signature strengths based on how you feel when you use them.

Caution: be careful when taking the survey. There is a concept in test-taking referred to as *social desirability responding*. This means that if a concept is being described that society dictates you "should" have or feel, you may respond "yes" or rate that feature as important to you when in reality it may not be at all. For example, "I am generous" sounds like something we should all aspire to in life. You certainly don't want to say that you are really a tightwad, due to feeling that there is never enough. So presented with this question and rating yourself on this trait, you may say, "Yes, I am very generous." That skews your results and what you will receive won't be an accurate picture of your strengths. These surveys are not shared with others, so it's important to be honest even on undesirable items.

   • With your identified strengths, find ways that these strengths can be incorporated into your life purpose, your recreational life, and your interpersonal relations. Make sure you are using them as much as possible so you feel like your authentic self. List them here:

Task #4.

What are you attracting right now? Look around you and pay attention to what is there. List the undesirable things in order to know what to focus your attention *away* from.

What would you like to attract? This is where your definiteness of purpose comes in; you will work on attracting all the success or happiness that is involved in the purpose you have defined. I assume that you would also like to attract good friends and a good mate, if you don't already have one. Good health is another option. Make these desires become real by only focusing on having them. Behave as though you already have them, in order to attract them.

An example would be:

> **Focus:** I want a new job and will focus on obtaining one. I will look in the paper, explore possibilities on the Internet, check with other companies in my field, make a new resume and fill out five applications per week until I get the job I would prefer. I will network with friends and attend public meetings where I can meet and connect with others who work in my chosen field. I will study what companies look for in the job position I want and strive to accomplish these qualities. I will think of nothing else and allow no limiting beliefs to take over.

> **Law of Attraction:** I am only thinking of my new job. I can picture myself in this position, how it will feel, and the types of people I will be around. I am thinking of what I will do with my new paycheck and planning my future accordingly.

> Repeat this exercise with all your limiting beliefs in order to set them off track and move onto your new path to happiness and success.

Task #5. Write down a couple of the questions that you repeatedly ask yourself. Are they good ones or bad ones, according to the definition in the section, "Asking the Right Questions." If they're bad ones, replace them now with some better ones that lead to your purpose and positive focus. Always ask your brain the right things to get good answers.

Task #6. With your newly identified purpose that you have decided upon, write down five goals that need to be achieved on the path to that purpose. Do them as soon as possible, then list five more, and so on. Just doing the first five will make you feel better already. Make daily, weekly and monthly goals to keep yourself moving in that direction.

Task #7. Go over the personality traits discussed and do a reality check of yourself. Be honest and work on those you feel might not be your strong points right now. Practice not having a RBF, the Resting *BIT@#* Face—something that can immediately turn others off and away.

Lose the Fear

*"My life has been filled with terrible
misfortunes; most of which never happened."*
—MICHEL EYQUEM DE MONTAIGNE

No self-help program would be complete without addressing the topic of *fear.* I am placing it in its own category and as a stand-alone Step and part of the Dysfunction Interrupted program because that is how important acknowledging and dealing with fear is. With your cognitive work and new language and Advanced Thinking Skills in place, you are now ready to take on the heavy stuff. And that is exactly what fear is, *the heavy stuff.* It prevents you from having a full enjoyable life; traps you in bad jobs and bad relationships; stops you from reaching your full potential; and keeps you on the sidelines while others go on to grab the gusto. There are different types of fear and different ways in which they limit you. Remember this: *fear will limit you.*

When you ask truly successful and happy people if they're ever afraid, they will almost always respond with a yes!

You are now ready to eliminate limiting yourself because you will learn another "secret." That secret is that the fear never goes away. There will always be some fear lurking about, that is part of life. When you ask truly successful and happy people if they're ever afraid, they will almost always respond with a yes! They're afraid of the exact same things that you are. This may be the fear of pushing themselves, the fear of what will come next, the fear of public speaking, the fear of failing, or the fear of being ridiculed. *All the same stuff.* The difference between them and someone who remains stuck and depressed is that they experience the fear and don't allow it to stop them. They push through the fear and come out on the winning end of it.

The Comfort Zone

Change is scary and change related to growth in particular. It requires that you push yourself beyond your comfort level, leaving your little cocoon of life that you have established. No matter how miserable you may be, you at least are familiar with your misery and managing it as you currently know how. Launching into new territory brings about many doubts and can even produce down-right terror.

Whenever you try to leave your comfort zone, you may have a little voice inside telling you discouraging types of things. The messages can include:

> *What are you doing? You can't possibly succeed as you are lazy and too dumb.*
>
> *No one would want to hear you talk. Your parents never listened to you so why would anyone else want to?*
>
> *You're "too fat" to do that or "too ugly."*
>
> *You will fail or waste money or lose money or hurt yourself.*
>
> *Be happy with what you have.*

Hopefully by now you have put the lid on some of that with the new language skills you're using and your new and positive words. However, I bet when it comes to your fears, that voice is a little stronger because it's been there the longest and is the most deeply seated.

Break on Through

Knowing that we all experience fear and doubt puts you in the company of the masses! However, fear doesn't have to be in your driver's seat. It can ride shotgun and propel you along renamed as drive or ambition. It can ride in the back seat and just grumble along like Miss Daisy. Or it can be towed behind the car as an afterthought because there was no room for it elsewhere.

The late Susan Jeffers, PhD, wrote books and developed workshops on the subject of fear. Her books are as timely today as when she first published them in 1987. Her best-selling title, *Feel the Fear and Do It Anyway* is absolutely the last resource you'll need in this department. I urge you to read her materials or attend a workshop based on her works—it's that valuable. Within this Step, I'm going to introduce you to some of the ideas put forth in her work.

Fears are only available in so many forms.

The only way you move beyond the fear is to do whatever it is you are afraid of and prove to yourself that it is not that scary. Is it something you can get used to? Or more often than not, you will find that your fear was blown all out of proportion because you really didn't know what the activity would be like. Having these fears that limit you is not a psychological problem with a diagnosis that requires medication or years of therapy. What it requires is that you examine and name the fear, understand why you have it and what it means to you and then move through it by performing the behavior anyway. There is nothing wrong with you; you just need the skill base to overcome your fears. Just like you may have needed the skill base associated with Advanced Thought and Cognitive Work. This is simply another area to learn and put to use.

Fears are only available in so many forms. There is being afraid of things that are unfortunate and can happen to us, like illness, death of a spouse, loss of money, natural disasters, or war. Let's call these "personal fears." Then there are those fears that are about doing something, such as going to school, changing jobs, driving ourselves around, and other things of that nature. I call these "procedural fears." If you look closely, both of these types of fears represent a number of things. Fear of rejection, fear for our personal safety, fear of success or failure, being vulnerable, loss of image or looking foolish in front of others, or being taken advantage of. It is easier to study fear when we break it down like this. It goes from being this big ambiguous monster to something clearly defined and manageable that already feels much better.

Personal fears are things that you really cannot change or predict, and worrying about them constantly is a waste of time and suffering. You will suffer enough when they really do happen, so why not wait till then? Sure, you can prepare to some extent for natural disasters, but then it is totally out of your hands. Procedural fears require a plan in place to learn or master the procedure. You need a plan if driving yourself somewhere is a fear for you or if you are returning to school later in life.

What if you wanted to go to school … it could be for a degree, a special training to advance your career or to learn new skills … it could be for anything. You would locate the school that has the program you want, visit the campus, work out the financial piece, and then start attending! If you require special assistance, there is always an office or department that will work with you on that. You then allocate a certain amount of time to study to ensure success.

If you take your school goal one step at a time and think of it as a process, like anything else, it becomes doable. It may be scary for a bit, but the rewards will outweigh the scariness. Here they are twofold. There is the personal gratification that you will receive from not only mastering your fear, but also from attending school and working toward whatever your goal is.

In *Feel the Fear and Do it Anyway,* Dr. Jeffers points out,

> At the bottom of every one of your fears is simply the fear that you can't handle whatever life may bring you.

Think about it. What you are actually thinking is, "I can't handle illness," "I can't handle making a fool of myself," "I can't handle a divorce or failure or being rejected." Actually, you *can* handle it, and you will handle it if you have to do so.

Now, think of some event where something unpredictable happened and you handled it, like rushing the dog to the vet or taking care of your child when he or she was sick. You have probably handled many things in life that you aren't giving yourself credit for. You may be engaging in the thought distortion called minimizing, as you learned in Step 2, *Cognitive-Based Work.*

Susan Jeffers identified what she believed to be the five truths about fear:

1. The fear will never go away as long as you continue to grow.
2. The only way to get rid of the fear of doing something is to go out and do it.
3. The only way to feel better about myself is to go out and do it.
4. Not only am I going to experience fear whenever I am on unfamiliar territory, but so is everyone else.

5. Pushing through fear is less frightening than living with the underlying fear that comes from a feeling of helplessness.

So, given that you are going to feel fear, it is your job to decide where it sits in your life. Does it drive the bus or ride along with you? Fear attempts to derail you not only in day-to-day personal life, but also in relationships and in your work life too. You get to choose how to deal with it.

Dealing with the "What Ifs"

Another feature of fear is that you find yourself confronted with the **"what ifs."** These are little fear-based characters that come out every time you go to make a decision. You are probably familiar with those characters that live in your mind and vocabulary. They go along with what was examined in Step 2 having to do with the distortions of thought. The *what ifs* come out with your fortune-telling and crystal ball including:

"What if he rejects me?"

"What if she leaves me?"

"What if I am poor?"

"What if I lose that job?"

"What if I am turned down for that job?"

"What if people laugh at me?"

"What if I pass out while I am talking?"

"What if I turn red and have a panic attack?"

"What if I drive in the wrong direction?"

"What if I can't learn to drive at all?"

"What if I never meet anyone else?"

"What if I get lost?"

"What if I lose money?"

"What if I am made fun of?"

"What if I look stupid?"

Does any of this sound familiar? YIKES!

The problem with the "what ifs" is that they are so scary few want to look for the answer. They are also the wrong kind of questions to be asking yourself as you have just learned in Step 4, *Advanced Thinking Skills.*

But let's take "What if I drive in the wrong direction?" as an example of a question to work through. Well, if you do, you would then get lost. If you are lost, you would call someone and get directions, use your GPS on your mobile, look at your map and see where you screwed up, or go into a store and ask someone for directions. One of those options will put you back on course. So that is it. Worst case scenario is that you are late to wherever you are going or you do not make it at all. The cell phone takes care of notifying the party involved and you go from there with rescheduling or whatever. Not the end of the world by any means, but if you don't go there, all you are thinking is, "I am going to get lost and that is scary." It is like watching a movie and then putting your hands over your eyes at the really scary part.

> **Every time you experience even a small success of breaking free of fear, it builds your self-esteem.**

In real life, you need to look at the scary part in your projections to see if it will really be that scary. You also need to remember that you can create your own ending, with the hero or heroine (you) having a great outcome as opposed to a gruesome one. That's what the thought distortion of catastrophizing revealed in Step 2.

Fear-Based Thinking

If you relate fear to pain, you will move away from it, and this is natural. You have to then redefine your fear to mean something else. What if you redefined it as a challenge, or a task to be overcome? Then you may move toward it, not away. If you are moving toward it or bringing it with you, you are allowing yourself to get your life in order and move out of your limiting habits. Every time you experience even a small success of breaking free of fear, it builds your self-esteem. There is no better way to feel better quickly than to accomplish something along this line.

As long as you let fear run the show, you will never break free and become the person you were meant to be. If you look deep inside, you will probably be able to see that some of your reasoning is actually *fear-based thinking.* Consider the following examples:

"The job market is bad so I can't look for another position. It would be a waste of time."

> **Real fear =** I will not be hired and will feel **rejection or humiliation,** which I don't like. Also, possible **failure.**

"I'm not going to get a divorce because all men are the same anyway, and I may as well keep this one."

> **Real fear =** I will be alone forever. I will experience **rejection.** I will find that I am unlovable and do not belong anywhere. The **financial** change may change my lifestyle.

"I am not going to drive because there is enough pollution in the air without me adding to it."

> **Real fear =** I will not be able to learn to drive and someone will **ridicule** me. **I will fail. I will harm myself.**

High Level and Low Level Decisions

The "what ifs" and fear affect the personality trait of being able to make decisions quickly and effectively. This trait takes some confidence to build and is important for success as discussed in the previous Step. If you think about it, the inability to make a decision, or the habit of doubting yourself, falls also in the fear category. You are afraid that you will make the wrong decision or screw up something irreversibly. Or you have learned from your parents that your thinking is somehow off so you resist making decisions or you take forever in fear of ridicule or failure.

Not surprisingly, this "fear" affects your day-to-day life, as well as in your work environment. Sometimes you just rely on others to make your decisions, thinking they will do a better job. Dependency is one of the undesirable effects that can result from fear.

Always ask yourself if you are making the decision out of fear or making the best decision based on facts at hand.

There are two kinds of decisions that you are faced with on a regular basis: **low level** decisions and those considered **high level.** The low level ones do not matter—what to eat for dinner or movie to see— just pick something and go with it. There is no right or wrong, and in the big picture, it doesn't matter at all anyway. Next year, you will only remember that you either saw such and such a movie or you did not. The things that matter such as job decisions, partner choice and finances are important, and you should gather all the information or research possible in order to make the best decision and then make it.

Always ask yourself if you are making the decision out of fear or making the best decision based on facts at hand. The decision may still turn out to be a dud for whatever reason. The job may not be as you had hoped or was not as advertised, and you will wish you had not made that choice. But that is not the end of things. That doesn't mean you are stuck in that job forever. Just as you changed jobs before you will change again. You will use your knowledge that you obtained from the less than desirable job and use it to get the next job. Decision-making is best seen as a path, not a dead-end street. There is not a person alive who hasn't made a decision that turned out less than ideal and had to revisit it. Learn from it and go on.

I always try to look at a worst case scenario, along with the information I have gathered, when making an important decision. I go with my decision if I am not bringing harm to anyone and can handle the worst case scenario I create when I look past my fear. If it is a mistake, I then have to make more decisions and the process starts over. Life is a process.

Fear and Relationships

Fear also inserts itself into your relationships, with the result of wreaking havoc on your emotional well-being. If you think back to the material learned having to do with attachment, you will also see where fear plays a role. Aren't the behaviors having to do with attachment in some ways protecting you from personal rejection by loved ones? Aren't they the learned behaviors and reactions to previous encounters with others that proved to be less than stellar in their ways of interacting with you?

Those early encounters actually affect bonding and future attachments and can be viewed as having their roots in fear. Individuals with a **secure attachment** style expect to have relationships and have confidence that these relationships will go reasonably well. They do not spend a lot of time fearing what will happen if there is no relationship or if the partner leaves.

Individuals with the **anxious attachment** style are constantly afraid of the relationship ending. Every piece of personal interaction between them and their partners is examined for possible clues that the relationship is over. They want to be the ones who leave, not the ones who get left. Relationships for these individuals are often very painful, just on a day-to-day basis, as they live in fear of it ending.

Avoidant individuals have most likely been hurt by others in bonding situations to the extent that they do not even try anymore. Or the avoidant persons will have adopted poor interpersonal skills that they feel leave them in control of the relationships they do enter.

Trusting others means exposing yourself or being vulnerable, which was identified as one of the basic fears. The very act of trying to start a relationship puts you at risk for ridicule, rejection and failure. When you have learned that others are not to be trusted through their poor behavior toward you in the past, you use this as validation of your fear. By avoiding relationship behaviors or behaving in ways that you feel minimize your risk, you are attempting to protect yourself from these negative feelings. Seems logical but it's wrong. What happens is that you are so busy protecting yourself that you then miss the enjoyable parts of life and relationships.

Fears are everywhere—the fear of being hurt, being rejected, being on your own, being lied to, and the fear of loss of financial security. You might fear the loss of a job if someone isn't telling you the truth about your performance, or being made a fool of if your partner is cheating.

You may become hypervigilant or always on the lookout (remember Boy Scout Brain?). Caretaking behavior boils down to the fear of being inherently unlovable. But your efforts to find and control any of these occurrences represents wasted time and energy. You could find the perfect partner to attach to and trust, just to have him or her hit by a bus or killed in a freak accident. You could think you have found your soul mate, just to find out that he or she was a polygamist with multiple families and was good at hiding that fact. You can never control for all the possible variables; you will drive yourself into misery.

All you can control is how you think about things. You have to live and enjoy for the moment, and when and if something bad happens, deal with it then. Choose the best partner you can find, and then put your all into it. If it goes south due to a bad choice or just bad behavior on the part of your partner, then move on knowing you did the best you could. Perhaps the other person just wasn't capable of a relationship or you were wrong for each other. Things are going to happen; you can't control for all of it. People may lie; people may cheat. Deal with it when it happens, not years before.

Remember how those constant worry thoughts affect your body, as in our equation:

$$T = PR$$

Thought = Physiological Response

Fear is extremely limiting. It can become all-encompassing as it envelopes your life if you allow it to.

In my decades of working with men and women, I believe **Fear** is the number one problem we face. In the Appendix, I've identified several experts and their books on a variety of topics including *fear*. Certainly not exhaustive, but an excellent sampling to understand.

Tasks for Step 5: Lose the Fear

Task #1 *What do you fear?* List at least three of your fears now:

Task #2 *Break them down into* procedural *versus* personal *fears.*

Task #3 *What can you put in place or plan for in order to work through the fears that are procedural?* Can you break down the event into small steps and set goals and time-lines to reach for? If so, do it now.

Task #4 If you identified some personal fears, think about whether they can be controlled for. Chances are you will come up with "No" for that answer. I like what ° suggests in this area. Try this. Repeat to yourself that you can handle it if it happens. You will have to handle it if it happens. You will get help handling it if it happens. Then let it go till it happens.

Task #5 *Have you ever experienced a failure that you're afraid of repeating?*

What happens if you do fail? List some events that you have considered to be failures and reexamine them to see if they're accurately classified as such. Did you learn from these events, and are you now able to apply that information to a new setting?

Task #6 *Can you replace a "what if" question in your life with a better question?* For example: "What if I never feel better?" Replace it with "How can I go about feeling better?"

Enrichment

> *"The most important thing is to enjoy your*
> *life—to be happy—it's all that matters."*
> —AUDREY HEPBURN

Enrichment starts the journey of you becoming the person you really want to be, and were meant to be. It means living a full and rewarding life, warts and all. It means adding all the fun and exciting things into your life that you desire. It also means doing all the things that define who you are and what your interests and personality are about.

As you add these things to your already more advanced thinking skills, you will finally really come alive and experience life. With the help of your new ways of thinking, you will immediately see the negative things begin to dissipate and be replaced with more positive events and emotions. As you strive to experience positive emotions, they will negate the negative ones. You'll begin to immediately choose the positive over the negative, as this feels better, and we as humans want to feel good.

Your parents may not have known how to instill correct thinking patterns or feelings of safety in you. Few dysfunctional families are focused on your enrichment needs. If you are suffering, you

> It's really not enough just to get through your day; you need to get through your day with excitement and in the best form you can.

don't believe that joy is even possible. It just hasn't been in your personal radar until now when you decided to interrupt the dysfunction that is now in your life.

A Closer Look

Enrichment, as defined here, involves finding the fun, rewarding and fulfilling things in life that define you—all components of the Dysfunction Interrupted program. Once they're identified, you start adding them to your life as frequently as possible. It also involves understanding the concepts of *gratification* and *spiritualism* and learning how both of these benefit you overall. This is a further switch of focus and mindset that works wonders and you'll feel the excitement start to build! So now you'll not only be thinking better, you'll be surrounding yourself with fun, as well as finding deeper, more long-lasting positive emotions.

It's really not enough just to get through your day; you need to get through your day with excitement and in the best form you can. It's the only way that you achieve real happiness and fulfillment.

> Happiness and the fulfillment of the true you are counter to depression.

When you add enrichment to your life, you become a person who is effective and provides yourself with happiness and a good balance of life experiences. No one is born to be miserable. That no one includes you.

This Step will provide you with a knowledge base about yourself that will help you get started in expanding your horizons. This is the really fun part. Most of the annoyances have been dealt with, and your major life purpose is hopefully on its way to the forefront of your mind. In order to completely round you out and make you happy, let's begin to fill your time with things that uplift you, enlighten you, make you happy, and make you laugh.

Please don't think that enrichment is a luxury. It is not. Enrichment is *essential* to your well-being, and something that is also not stressed enough in traditional therapy. Happiness and the fulfillment of the true you are counter to depression. It's just as important, if not more, as understanding maladaptive patterns. There's nothing that says you have to dwell in problems and sadness constantly. In fact, you want to behave in ways that are contrary to that. Your entire identity need not be about depression or some emotional illness. You can have those and still pursue interests and goals.

When I have skeptical clients, I encourage them to understand that sometimes you can just let the behavior come first, then the attitudes and beliefs. Just like with dieting, if we have a sweet tooth, we're not going to wake up one day hating cookies and doughnuts. It's just not going to happen if you are a cookie and doughnut lover. But if you stop eating them and begin to lose weight, you realize, "Oh, that works really well!" Then you become a believer. Losing weight starts to feel better than cookies taste!

Where would you be if you hadn't spent so much time suffering the same dysfunctional dynamics over and over? It's time to go there now. Don't feel this is unattainable because you're now married, have children, or are in a job or a location that is less than ideal. You can still develop yourself around these things. As you expand and develop yourself, you will actually find doors opening that you didn't even know existed. Those doors may prove to be your answer to current circumstances that you would prefer to change. In pursuing your enrichment needs, you may meet your next business partner, employer or romantic partner. Opportunities abound when you are open to them.

With all your right thinking skills in place and your personality fine-tuned, you're now ready to join the world and fully participate! In fact, you owe it to yourself and your family to be your best you.

That way, you won't repeat the same family dynamics that were so destructive. How will you teach your children better if you aren't convinced better can happen? You have to be a role model of well-being.

Enrichment Exercises

So what do you love? What makes you smile? What makes you happy? Chances are you might not even know. You will have to go find it. This is fun. First, sit and think of what made you laugh or happy as a child. Was it a hobby or craft in school? Was it being around pets or animals? Was it being in the woods or around water? Was it reading a certain kind of book or playing a certain game or sport? Were you athletic? If so, are you now?

What makes you smile?

What makes you happy?

This is an exercise that has been consistently embraced and effective with my clients and is one that takes some thought. Jot down these things now, as many as you can think of. Then think through each phase of your life, and remember if there were activities that piqued your interest. Disregard cost and practicality right now. You are busy dreaming. What makes you smile?

For the second exercise, what I want you to do is go to a bookstore or library and look over the magazine racks, then the book racks on different topics. Pretty much anything in the world that you may be interested in is just a rack away. Yes, it's easy to go to the Internet for instant answers, but not for this exercise. Why I want you to go to a physical location is for the immediate visual tied with the ability to touch and feel. There is a different experience when you can hold your dream in your hands.

Pick up a magazine or book of a hobby or topic that you think may interest you, and read a few pages. If it's a magazine, look at the ads.

Does it excite you and make you want to look more or does it bore you? If it bores you, put it down and move to the next topic. There are hobbies galore, spiritual, and travel and sports magazines. Pick a hobby, a religion, a new career path, an intellectual pursuit. Go all out and redesign yourself in the bookstore. You don't even have to buy all the books, just sit down with them and look at the topics you have chosen. Write down all the topics you decided were interesting to you, even if they seem farfetched. When you return home, study them further on the Internet.

Now you're on the way to being the real you. For example, you may come out interested in becoming a Buddhist who knits, cooks ethnic foods, and likes to study the stars. You may decide that you're interested in converting to Judaism, going deep-sea diving, and becoming a photographer in your spare time. How about taking up an interest in fitness and the cinema or opera? Joining a wildlife or environmental group? The possibilities are endless. Your imagination becomes your guiding light and force.

The Next Move

Now decide how you can incorporate these things into your life, given your time, finances, etc. It *can* be done. Maybe all you can do right now is learn about the new hobby, and take part in online discussions and blogs. Well, you'll start to make friends who do what you want to do; just begin to immerse yourself and you'll see things start to happen. Remember to focus on it with all you've got! You can add one thing right now to get the idea. If you're a depressed or anxious person, you should feel something "click" almost immediately; studies show that novelty stimulates the "feel good" chemicals of the brain.

It's important not to get bogged down in adding too much at once; this is not designed to be a chore. Don't go buy expensive equipment you can't afford. Find a doable affordable thing and start right now. The time you're not researching depression or some other mental health issue can be spent researching something fun. This also opens up the doors to meeting like-minded people with whom you have something in common. Chances are, you would like to replace or put in place some rewarding relationships. This is a good time and place to start looking.

Gratification vs. Pleasure

This concept is critical to your well-being, and it's again one that doesn't always find itself in mainstream psychotherapy. I'm including it here in our Enrichment Step as it relates to finding the most rewarding activities possible. This has been an area of interest and research in a relatively new field of psychology, Positive Psychology, founded and developed by Martin Seligman, PhD, of the University of Pennsylvania. Dr. Seligman has written several books having to do with happiness and well-being, including his two latest best-sellers, *Flourish* and *Authentic Happiness*. I encourage you to read both in order to obtain a complete understanding and mastery of these ideas.

The concept of gratification is different from that of pleasure, but they are often considered to be synonymous. Pleasure involves feeling good or enjoying something for a moment, the immediate sensory experience. For example, while eating food, you may feel pleasure at that moment as you enjoy your meal. Or an afternoon of lying around the pool may be pleasurable. But neither of these activities produces long-lasting feelings or enhances your overall well-being; they're passive activities like watching television.

> **The concept of gratification is different from that of pleasure, but they are often considered to be synonymous.**

Gratification comes from doing something that brings you deep satisfaction, builds your self-esteem, and may produce feelings of connectedness to the world. It comes from activities that actively engage you, where you are using your strengths or interests to the point that you lose track of time. That may sound difficult, but it's not. It's actually very simple and will come naturally to you when you find the right activity.

Gratification comes from a feat well done or a job well done. Hiking a challenging mountain gives you gratification when you use your abilities to master the trail. It can also come from giving, leaving a name or a legend behind, or contributing in a positive way to someone or a group of someones. Gratification doesn't come about from passively staring at the TV or loitering around doing nothing. Reading a great book can produce gratification, whereas reading a "fluff" book can produce some pleasure or kill time.

Developing one of the activities you found of interest in the bookstore is likely to produce gratification for you. When you're fully engaged in something, your mind isn't concerned with being depressed or anxious or anything else. It's completely absorbed in whatever it is that you're doing. Research actually shows that individuals engaging in activities that produce gratification are relieved of depression faster than those who don't include this in their treatment. They also are less likely to suffer from relapses.

Remember your definition of purpose and your focus? As you move toward those, you are also likely to find gratification as you engage in tasks and activities that bring about your dreams.

Gratification is also found in activities that contribute to others. Again, this doesn't have to be a time-sucker, and if you have children, they can certainly participate. This is a concept that will benefit them to learn young. Can you do neighborhood cleanup or nursing home visits or participate in some type of community service? Maybe through your church or children's school? What about just helping an elderly neighbor? It could be something as seemingly simple as picking up a few extra bags of cat or dog food for the shelter and delivering it. Anywhere you can give and pitch in makes you feel like part of the bigger whole. That appears to be essential to gratifying the human spirit.

Spiritualism

This is our last concept pertaining to Enrichment. Spiritualism doesn't mean that you have to participate in organized religion, if that is unappealing to you. Just find a philosophy of life that makes sense to you and try it for a while. It may or may not be the religion you grew up with. Research has shown

> As you move toward your purpose and focus, you are also likely to find gratification as you engage in tasks and activities that bring about your dreams.

that individuals who have a spiritual or philosophical belief system in place suffer less emotional difficulty, have better self-esteem, and report greater life satisfaction than those who don't.

You may choose to explore this while doing the earlier bookstore exercise or you may want to make a separate trip focusing only on this topic. You can further research those philosophies and spiritual paths that interest you on the Internet. This could even include having daily sayings sent to you from the belief of your choice from a website called *BeliefNet.com*. While some individuals take comfort in the idea of an all powerful God as in most organized religions, some people prefer the idea of a path or philosophy to follow for life such as Buddhism or Taoism. Others believe in an infinite intelligence or energy source that offers guidance or is part of the world and all of us. It really doesn't matter what you choose. It simply helps build faith, provides comfort, helps you to connect with like-minded individuals, and guides you to your ultimate life satisfaction.

Whatever you choose, make it a part of your daily life. You can do this through actions, prayers, meditations, interacting with others of the same belief, or attending services. In this busy world, you may find that interacting on the Internet with a group of your spiritual choice is all you can manage right now, and that is fine.

Tasks for Step 6: Enrichment

Task #1 *List the things you liked to do as a child.* Can you remember losing yourself in some activity where you lost track of time and hated for it to end? What did you like to study? What interests did you have?

Task #2 *What do you like to do now?* Are you allocating time each day or week to do it? If you are not, look at your schedule right now and find a place for it. Maybe it only makes sense right now to engage in discussions or learn about it on the Internet. That is fine but schedule some time for it.

Task #3 *(1) Do the bookstore or library exercise described above within this Step.* List here what you come up with. It may take a few trips. Try to choose a hobby or sport, an intellectual or cultural interest such as history, music or art, and a spiritual interest if you don't already have one.

Have fun defining you. (2) Next, schedule them into your week, day
or month.

Task #4 *Identify one of the activities or add another that is going to provide
you with gratification, not just pleasure.* List a couple of potentials here,
and then investigate whether they are actually gratifying or not by doing
them as soon as possible. Keep searching till you find one or more that fit
the bill.

Boundary Setting & Relationship Overhaul

"This above all: to thine own self be true."
—WILLIAM SHAKESPEARE, *HAMLET*, ACT 1

Boundary setting is the next skill you will add to your growing repertoire of feel good behaviors. As you can see, your skills build on each other and allow you to shape your life. The purpose of having boundaries is to protect and take care of you. They define how you want to be treated and how you want to live in relationships. When you honor your own boundaries, you are living true to you.

One of the challenges that most face today is in letting others know when they're behaving in ways that violate one's boundaries. That means yours. Have you thought about them? Clearly identified what is a button pusher for you?

Lack of boundaries is anxiety-provoking in that it usually means you have little time for yourself. Without boundaries, you are under the constant stress of reacting to things that aren't necessarily part of your ideal existence. You may be confused over what is okay in relationships and how someone is treating you. You know something is wrong but aren't sure how to correct it. You may constantly find yourself allowing others to use up your time with their problems or issues, and as a result, not have time for yourself or your own family. You may not have time for your enrichment needs if you do not have personal boundaries in place.

In the two Steps pertaining to Advanced Thinking and Enrichment, you have defined or started to define for yourself what you want out of life, what your purpose is, and what you want to spend your time doing. These things that you have chosen and are focused on are the things that should now be consuming your time—not emotionally unhealthy family members or friends or people who drain you. You also cannot participate on every committee out of a desire to please or the inability to say no. You're still in the process of defining *you*.

Think of this as buying a pet; you need to learn how to treat him. What does he like and not like? What is good for him and what isn't? What do you feed him to keep him healthy? Who do you allow him near? Certainly not Aunt Margaret who hates pets and may hurt him! You teach others how to treat him, and if they refuse to obey your rules, you stop letting them play with him.

You're also not going to allow your pet around someone who makes fun of him and causes him to feel shame. He has to rest, he has to play, and he needs a little quiet time when he gets overstimulated. He needs not to form friendships with lizards, worms, snakes or other creatures that are very unlike him; there probably wouldn't be anything satisfying about the relationship. He may like other puppies, he may like kittens and even a hamster or monkey; however, there are other life forms he just won't get and they won't get him. He draws natural boundaries by snubbing them. He instinctively knows they may not be good to be with. Your pet has set up a few boundaries.

Boundaries are good and protect who you are. They define you. Boundaries are healthy and definitive; they give you peace and reduce stress and depression. By working through the seventh Step in *Dysfunction Interrupted*, imagine you now become your beloved and protected pet.

Delving Deeper

Personal boundaries are guidelines, rules or limits that a person creates to identify what are reasonable, safe and permissible ways for other people to behave in his or her presence. They also spell out how the person—*you*—will respond when someone steps outside those limits. In defining yourself, you draw boundaries that pertain to your physical self, your time and energy, your mental or intellectual beliefs, and your spiritual self.

Just as you don't want someone to touch you or be in your personal space too close, you don't want someone pressing their religion or ideas upon you too strongly. It may be fine for them to present their thoughts, but you know when it becomes uncomfortable because they are too intense. It's the same thing when someone may try to convince you that you should join the PTA or something you don't really have time for. Another type of boundary you draw is not being interrupted by co-workers in the middle of your projects or friends calling you at work. All day you encounter potential boundary issues. It's normal.

When you lack boundaries, as you may if you haven't been taught how to set them, you will feel as though you're reacting to everything around you. If there isn't a well-defined "you" in place, you'll be bouncing all around. Think about an old pinball machine. To play it, you would set the ball loose pulling on the spring knob. The ball would bounce around like crazy off everything in its way. There is no clear path defined for the ball—and getting any type of high score was usually just lucky.

When you're clearly defined, it saves you a lot of trouble.

Now think of yourself as that pinball— those things that get in your way are some of life's obstacles. You haven't created a clear definition of self to get you through the barriers that get thrown in your path. When you're clearly defined, it saves you a lot of trouble. There are many doors and obstacles you don't even have to deal with, because your boundary has already made them off limits.

Others' Reactions

We all have to set boundaries in order to have healthy relationships with healthy people who make us feel good. Once you set *your boundaries*, there are going to be the conscientious objectors in your life who don't like the new you or your new boundaries. After all, they were the ones benefitting from your lack of them in the first place. They will act out, threaten to leave you, call you selfish, attempt to make you feel guilt and fear. None of these tactics can allow you to interfere with your progress. Boundaries are a critical component in living a balanced life, something that you are choosing to do.

Keep in mind that you don't cause others to feel a certain way. You shouldn't take ownership for others' feelings and reactions. If they have misunderstood your intention, it's fine to clear that up. But let's say that you have drawn a boundary and they fight it—they tell you it's unfair or makes them feel rejected. Don't take ownership to their sense of unfairness—it's their issue, not yours. Maybe you have said, "I need to go to bed because I have to get up for work," and that person feels rejected because you won't stay on the phone another hour. They're the ones being disrespectful to you, attempting to break your boundary, and that is their issue. You didn't make them feel that way; that is a product of their own lack of boundaries. Your job is to stick up for yourself, go to bed, and forget about it.

Here are the parameters in these cases—there are many possible examples. Stick with boundary setting if:

- You're being true to yourself.
- You're taking care of yourself.
- You know your intent isn't to harm anyone.
- You're not doing anything harmful.

If you make an error by mistake, you can correct it later. In all likelihood, you're not going to do anything life-altering.

If someone in your life can't handle a healthy boundary, then that person is not acting *in your best interest*. If it's family, you may not be able to just cut them out of your life. However, you can certainly stick to your boundaries and ignore their undermining strategies and manipulations as best as possible by limiting your interaction.

Boundaries That Must Be Honored ... No Exceptions

Some boundaries are rigid and never to be broken or violated ... not even a little.

These include:

"It's never okay to be physically violent with me. Period."

"It's not okay to ever call me derogatory names or say things that devalue me."

"It's not okay to do either of the above with my/our children."

Yes, these sound so obvious. But if you ask someone who has grown up in an abusive or dysfunctional home without boundaries related to this, these very basic premises are hard to assert. They grew up thinking that this is the way people do things; this is how people live. Or they feel they can't do better or don't deserve better. It's their *normal*.

These boundaries have to be actual lines drawn in the sand so to speak. They can never be violated if you are to be happy and in control of your life.

How to Set and Keep a Boundary

Boundary setting itself goes like this … Set the boundary and share with others in your life what will happen if they violate the boundary. Or you just set the boundary and keep it to yourself if you feel that sharing it will be to your detriment. For example, let's say you tell a very violent person that you're going to leave if they hit you again or that you're going to call the police. This may provoke an attack. Its better, in that instance, to get help from someone in advance, have a place to go, or just go there if the violence reoccurs and let the violent person then know what happened. The probability is that this person is so emotionally unwell that he or she is not able to participate in healthy boundary setting anyway.

If it's something not that drastic, such as someone who calls nightly during dinner, you may handle it like this:

"Would you mind calling at a different time? Six o'clock is our dinner hour and we like to share this time together as a family. We spend from six to seven o'clock together nightly."

What if the person violates it by calling the next night at the same time? You could say:

"Remember, our dinner time is from six to seven o'clock.
I won't be answering the phone anymore during that time
period. I would be glad to call you later in the evening."

If the person persists in calling at that hour, ignore the phone so he
or she gives up when you will not answer. You have protected your
time and it will feel good. You may want to reexamine keeping the
relationship, depending on how long it takes the person to give up
after you have clearly communicated your boundary. Is the relationship at all rewarding for you? Is it a two-way or a one-way street?

Give some careful thought to what the consequences will be if
someone violates a boundary. Don't use a consequence that hurts
you more than it does the other person. Also, don't threaten something that you can't follow through with or will possibly not follow
through with. The offender just learns to ignore you because he or
she knows you don't mean business. But do think it through and
choose a consequence that affects the other person.

Setting boundaries is not about controlling the other person or
manipulating him or her into a behavior. It's also not just a means
of making threats. The boundaries are there to protect you and
teach others how you want to be treated. Setting boundaries is a
process of taking responsibility for your own life.

Dysfunctional Homes and Boundaries

Boundaries are lacking in almost all dysfunctional families. They're
not taught, set, recognized or honored. The individuals from these
families then fear boundaries, believing that they will be viewed as
self-centered or hurtful to others. They may also believe that having
boundaries will cause rejection or conflict.

In dysfunctional families, there's a lack of knowledge of how to accurately identify a boundary and how to honor it in ways that reflect personal integrity and build healthy relationships. The purpose of setting boundaries is to protect, define and take care of yourself. You need to be able to share with people when they're treating you in ways that are unacceptable.

Examples of setting healthy boundaries:

- Please do not call after 9 P.M. as I/we go to bed early.

- Please do not call me with ongoing crises or drama. A psychologist is better suited to handle these—I'm not trained to help you. And, the information upsets me.

- Please do not share inappropriate information with our children.

- I don't want to be touched like that.

- Our children cannot visit you if you've been drinking. They certainly will not be riding with you in the car.

- I am not riding with you if you're drinking.

- Thank you for the invitation to your church, political meeting, etc. I am happy with my own beliefs right now and my time is too limited to add other activities. (Unless you're looking for other activities and it sounds interesting.)

- Thank you for thinking of including me but I really cannot take on any more things to do right now. I may be able to help in the future. (If asked to head up committees, etc., when you truly are overloaded already.)

- I make it a policy to not lend money as I feel that this can jeopardize relationships. Or simply say, "I do not have money that I can lend."

Boundaries and Loved Ones

If the boundary breaker is *your significant other*, such as a husband, wife, boyfriend or girlfriend, you have a couple choices. You can communicate this information to him/her and exercise your new boundary setting skills, or you can give couples counseling a try so that someone else will be explaining the concept to your partner. You have a tough choice to make if your mate isn't willing to go to couples therapy or undermines you and does not actively participate in your sessions. Most likely, you may have chosen this person when you weren't very healthy. He or she may not be very good for you.

Breaking up, especially a divorce, can be a difficult decision but I think it is sometimes necessary. Spending your life with someone who doesn't treat you well can affect both your mental and physical health. If you have children, this is a more difficult decision, and you should talk it over with a professional to make sure you have exhausted all possible avenues of keeping the family together. Even if it still results in a split, you have the peace of mind of knowing you tried everything in your power.

Boundaries with your *children* are another area that warrants your attention. Just as your parents may not have had boundaries or taught you about them, your children will not learn this if you don't teach it. Children should be taught the personal boundaries that most parents do teach, such as not letting others touch them and telling if they do. They also need to learn to respect boundaries set by the family in the form of rules. Boundaries give the children rules and define the family system for them. Behaviors that are okay and not okay are learned and reinforced, allowing children to understand the family and their role. Remember the problems stemming from being a "Free for All" family?

In addition, your children aren't your friends; you shouldn't tell them about your sex life or how rotten your partner is. This is inappropriate information sharing. Your children have *friends*; they need you to be *parents*. Understand that you are the parent; you do the teaching and the friendship part will come anyway. I will not belabor this point here, as there are many great parenting programs out there. Just remember to incorporate parenting boundaries into your life if you have children. One great resource on this topic is *Boundaries with Kids: How Healthy Choices Grow Healthy Children* by Henry Cloud and John Townsend. Children who are out of control are not pleasant to be around, and they cause incredible distress for the parent trying to contain them.

Boundaries and Holidays

Holidays will be the final topic in my discussion of boundaries. They can be great celebrations of boundary breaking! Holidays are like the national "boundary breakers free-for-all." These are the things they make movies out of. Foods are brought to your home that you may not want or object to for some reason. People who are difficult enough to deal with on the telephone may now be staying in your home for a few days. If you're a parent, gifts may be given to your children that you don't approve of. The intruders are telling you and the children things you don't want to know, and they're asking you about things that you don't want to share. Plus, they're giving you advice on running your life, home, etc. Worse than that, you may have family members or in-laws who are downright insulting or verbally abusive. The tips below are for all occasions but really help keep it together for the Holidays.

1. It is your house, you set the rules.

2. If your partner is not on board, making things difficult or full of conflict, and you haven't had time to work it out beforehand, then you'll have to set some inner boundaries

to get through. Inner boundaries are when you decide not to allow things to get to you; you distance yourself emotionally from the offenders. You just look at them and hear "blah blah blah" or the teacher voice from the Charlie Brown cartoons. You may envision a shield of some sort separating you from them. Your goal is to remain peaceful and enjoy your holiday. Remember **T = PR: Thought = Physiological Response.**

3. Decorate as you see fit, whatever you love looking at throughout the season. Never mind if it's the best or the brightest in the neighborhood; it's no good if the stress of doing it takes six years off your life. Put out Aunt Tillie's ghastly decoration she gave you last year, it will make her feel good, and you also, as you have taken the "high road." The very challenge of looking at it and knowing you are doing a good thing will give you gratification.

4. If gifts are given that you don't approve of, calmly wait until afterward and donate them to charity. If the gift giver finds out, you can simply remind them that they were told not to bring those sorts of things into your home. Make sure you have told them first; people cannot honor boundaries if they don't know what they are.

5. If foods are brought in that you wouldn't normally allow and you have children, just remind your kids that you don't eat those items. Then put them out anyway for the people who brought them. At the end of the meal, give them back to the givers to take home with them, reminding them that it will just go to waste in your home. Do this with a smile and thank them anyway. The goal is to feel good, not create a big deal. If they refuse to take the food home, just throw it away. Everything doesn't have to be a big battle.

6. If the offenders sit at the table or in your home and begin to insult you, you have a couple choices depending on the situation. If there are no children and you cannot make them go home, you can get up from the table and say, "I prefer to go to the movies than sit here and be insulted." Then go. You can also point out their behavior in case they think it's just a joke, with something like: "I prefer not to sit here and be insulted; is there another topic someone would like to discuss?"

   If by then your partner is not on board, the problem is deeper than the relatives. If they're your own relatives, it is usually easier to handle them. Tell them what they're doing is upsetting; you're not on Earth to be the brunt of their abuse. Add that you're not just extremely sensitive, and tell them they need to stop or there will be no more togetherness for the holidays. You would rather be in a dentist's chair than sitting there with them.

7. Picture yourself as an angel looking down on the situation; can you see yourself sitting there being made fun of or insulted? Can you see your face? Can you see the pack of jackals sitting there enjoying themselves at your expense? You have to protect yourself. Get up from the table and remove yourself from their presence. No one was put on Earth to put up with abuse from mean-spirited and/or ignorant individuals.

8. Your other choice if it is tolerable is to simply tune them out, and tune in to the part of the day that you're enjoying. Having the time off work, the food, the music, your own children, whatever brings you joy in that moment and allows you to look at them and just think, "What idiots!" If they're your partner's family, find something to do in another part of the house or go outside and do something.

If you know ahead of time that they are problematic, have activities planned that get you away or get them away. Arrange for your partner to take them to an activity, for a ride, or to play cards with them while you cook dinner to keep them out of your kitchen.

9. Remember, the goal of *Dysfunction Interrupted* is to put you in control of your life and the whole show. This is *your* life.

When you're clearly defined, it saves you a lot of trouble. There are many doors and obstacles that you don't even have to deal with. The reason? Because your boundaries have already made them off limits.

Tasks for Step 7: Boundary Setting and Relationship Overhaul

Task #1 *List your current boundaries in all areas.* Are there some boundaries that you need to set? Are there limits that you can set that will make you feel more defined and comfortable within yourself? Write those down now, along with who will be affected by them and what you expect his or her reaction to be.

Task #2 *List the names of the individuals who are boundary breakers in your life.*

Task #3 *List which boundaries they break on a regular basis.*

Task #4 *Come up with a clear definition of your boundary that they are breaking, and what the future consequences will be if they continue to be disrespectful of that boundary.* Write it down.

Task #5 *Now, think through your life without this person or persons, if they cannot respect your boundaries.* What changes? Are you going to be missing out on something or someone spectacular who cannot be replaced? Does this leave room for you to replace this person with someone you truly enjoy?

Task #6 *How can you make this process the most comfortable for yourself?* List your ideas here. They may include things such as fazing the person out by spending less and less time with him/her, as opposed to just cutting that person out immediately, and so on.

Task #7 *Are there certain situations that you routinely dread?* Examine them to see if you avoid them because you need to draw some boundaries pertaining to whatever it is. Some things are just boring or unpleasant and some things are unpleasant because you have allowed yourself to get into something you would rather not.

Body Basics

"Take care of your body. It's the only place you have to live." —JIM ROHN

No self-help plan is complete without addressing your physical body. The amazing machine that gets you through your day and life. You may question why this is important in a book that focuses on emotions. I assure you that it is all connected. How you nourish yourself is directly connected to how your brain works, as it requires appropriate fuel to work correctly. If all you eat is sugar or simple and processed carbohydrates (with the accompanying highs and lows), your brain is not going to be at maximum working capacity.

Your body requires certain things in order to have sustained energy and to convert energy to output. Blood sugar stabilizes your mood, and if it is out of whack, you feel out of whack as well. That is why balancing your proteins and carbohydrates is not only important—it is critical to your well-being. You wouldn't fill up the gas tank of your car with sugar and alcohol. How can you expect your body to run on it?

A Healthy Diet and a Healthy Weight

Utilizing your new thinking skills now gives you a different out-look on healthy diet and weight control. You have examined your questionable belief systems, and maybe there were some regarding weight and food that you included in the Tasks at the end of each Step. If you didn't assess them earlier in the cognitive Step, this is an ideal time to do it.

> *Do you believe that food is a comfort?*
>
> *Do you believe that you will always be heavy so there is no point in trying anything different?*
>
> *Do you believe you're ugly so you may as well be fat?*
>
> *Do you use food to self-soothe when you're feeling anxious or down?*
>
> *Have you failed with so many diets that you can't even imagine starting another?*

There are many ways that you can develop an unhealthy relationship with food, and chances are you have struggled with this. Your time management and busy life schedule may be dictating fast food or processed pre-packaged food that is full of chemicals.

So far, you have learned to switch your focus away from what you don't want. What's undesirable for you will now also include being overweight or unhealthy, so you are going to be focused on the goal of a healthy weight and the habit of fueling your body with nourishing food items. You and your thinking have new words and new ways of using your words that promote success, as opposed to repeated failure. So forget past efforts at weight control and proper diet, and learn to utilize your new skill base in this arena.

If you're overweight, you know that it can be depressing. Clothing choices are limited, activities can be limited, and most feel uncomfortable if weight gets too much out of control. People may even treat you differently. Studies show that medical doctors are even biased toward heavier people who they feel will not take control of their health as are some workplaces and job recruiters. Whether it is fact or fiction, the terms "lazy" and "ineffective" get assigned to those who carry excessive weight.

If you are unhappy with your body every day, it drains energy from you that could be put to better use. It makes those negative thoughts harder to push aside as they are present every time you look in the mirror. So please decide that this time you're going to succeed. You *will* have all the mental tools you need, and you are ready!

If you're on an antidepressant, antipsychotic or mood stabilizer, you may have a harder time losing weight. These medications tend to promote weight gain, since they interact with the part of your brain that craves carbohydrates and controls satiation. You might want to consult with your physician, if this is the case for you. Your physician may be able to change your medication to something that will not interfere with your efforts.

You've heard it a million times. Being in good physical shape requires two elements—*correct diet* and *exercise.* You may be groaning by now as you have studied these ad nauseam. It's not necessary for either of these parts of your plan to be a negative. Let's have a look at them instead using your new skill base. They're going to be part of your "feel good" plan.

Some Ideas to Try Out

Too much sugar and rich or processed carbohydrates cause blood sugar irregularities, and along with that comes mood shifts and lethargic feelings. Improper diet affects concentration and digestion, and it can lead to serious health concerns, such as high blood pressure and cardiac problems. When you eliminate such negative factors from your diet, your body is able to do more for you. With the proper fuel, the body can exercise better, think better and keep your mood more stable. You'll have much more energy.

All medical professionals and diet plans tend to agree that the best diet to follow for optimal health as well as weight loss is one with lean protein, fresh vegetables, whole rather than refined carbohydrates, some dairy, no or very little sugar or sugar substitutes, and moderate alcohol usage. There are hundreds of diet plans out there if weight loss is your goal.

You, on a Diet by Mehmet Oz, MD, and Michael Roizen, MD, is a book that I recommend. It contains all the information you'll need to choose healthy foods for your body and to lose weight. Figure out how many calories a day you need or what keeps you healthy using the tools from the book, and then give yourself a reasonable amount of time to make adjustments. If you need to drop some pounds, choose a realistic weight for you. The website *DoctorOz.com* also offers valuable related resources.

I personally have also utilized Weight Watchers Online (*Weight Watchers.com*) and its related meetings and programs. These are both very effective, and they teach you about portion control as well as all the other aspects of nutrition that you may need to learn. I like the online program as it allows me to do it from anywhere. You just keep track of your "points" daily on your computer. It also allows you to tally up points for exercise and track your weight and goals over time. It's relatively inexpensive per month and they run specials from time to time as incentives to sign up. You can investigate this further on the site. No attendance at meetings is necessary if you use the online version (but they do provide support that can be helpful), and you're given tools, such as restaurant and complete food guides, when you sign up.

Another diet plan that I followed for a while to see how it worked and how I felt was *The Paleo Diet* by Loren Cordain, PhD. It is also known as the caveman diet since it's a "back to basics" program. Both *The Paleo Diet* and *The Paleo Answer* describe this food plan. You'll also find basics about it on the website, *ThePaleoDiet.com*. There are other programs along this idea as well, however this just happened to be the one I studied.

I felt great and lost weight relatively quickly on the Paleo Diet. I didn't feel deprived of food and it wasn't a nuisance to follow. The main gist behind this plan is to eat mostly protein, vegetables and fruits, which your body knows how to process naturally. You also limit processed carbohydrates, which normally turn into fat—something you want to reduce. It doesn't get much simpler than

It's important to know what we humans were designed to eat, but not eat anything and everything.

that. Before processed foods were created, this is what people would have eaten, and the author has researched some of what early man ate. There are programs offered within the book for those who want to lose weight and for those who are just seeking a healthy eating style for life.

One last recommendation is *The Drop 10 Diet* by Lucy Danziger, editor-in-chief of *Self* magazine. The foods and food combinations are designed not just to help you lose weight but to promote healthy eating for a lifetime. She focuses on consuming the "superfoods" that are currently of great focus in the nutrition world, studied and promoted by the health experts. I also like that *Self* has a website with a variety of health and nutrition information as well as activities and challenges that the consumer can participate in. The plus is that it's presented in a format that is easily understood.

There are also many eating related applications or "apps" for the iPhone and iPad that can be downloaded under the category

"Health and Fitness." They will track foods, count calories, give you a workout to follow, and keep shopping lists of superfoods for you. They will sound alarms when it is time to eat and have snacks and so on. Some are free and some have a nominal charge. I find it helpful to read the reviews and see what others are saying before I buy any. If there are too many negatives, keep searching. You don't want to waste time fooling around with something that doesn't do what it says it will do or is too hard to use.

It's important to know what we humans were designed to eat, but not eat anything and everything. All living things are programmed to eat certain things for optimal performance, and they seem to know instinctively how to get it or hunt for it or whatever they need to do to feed themselves. This is a relatively simple concept, yet hours are spent agonizing over food and trying to figure things out. There are many choices and unfortunately some of the choices, although delicious, are terrible for you. Twinkies are not found in the wild.

If you have tried dieting countless times and failed, you could feel discouraged at this point. Just forget about your past attempts. Use the above recommendations to grocery shop and eat. It's all you need. Don't overwhelm yourself with expensive diets, complicated recipes and plans. Just get started and stick with a simplified diet outlined in the ones that I mentioned.

Try one of the above plans and commit to working with it for just one month. See if it works for you. Each offers something for everyone, and I don't believe you really need to look further to lose weight or eat healthier. They are based on good health and balanced nutrition using real food, and they teach you the skills you need so you're able to master the concepts and move forward. They're eating plans that you can live with forever. We want this to be simple so it doesn't interfere with your life anymore. If you find that you don't like the one you initially chose, do a different one.

Some remain thin even though they eat all sorts of things that would have the rest of us rolling out the door on a dolly cart. If you are one of these individuals (who appear outwardly in control of food issues), you still need to be aware of healthy eating. Are you overdosing on sugar or treats regularly? If so, it's likely to be impairing your brain functioning and energy levels as well. It may be affecting your mood or giving you that carbohydrate crash that occurs after a big pasta lunch. You may not be completing all the work you could, as you are nodding off in the afternoon. Remember, the goal is *to feel good.* If you are in this "lucky" category, you may need to eat a more balanced diet even if your goal isn't to lose weight.

Exercise Helps, Too

It really does work. The brain releases endorphins when you exercise; endorphins make you feel good. They help to balance out the stress hormones that are fighting to take over. It's that simple. If you've gotten off track with your fitness routine, it's time to get back on board. If you've never been much of an exerciser, it's time to start being one. Exercising will help you succeed with this program and with life. Just the act of beginning to exercise makes you feel in control.

Just *walk 20 to 30 minutes* on as many days as possible, if that's all you have time for. Exercise gives you a chance to clear your head. Having your body work for you makes you feel in control of yourself and part of the physical world. Your muscles need to move to work properly and to keep you from being weakened or injured easily.

Note: *Check with your doctor if you have health concerns that may prevent you from exercising, and if you plan to jump into something rigorous, then proceed with his or her blessing only.*

Exercising doesn't have to be boring. If walking isn't your thing, do a dance class or dance DVD, yoga, Pilates, swimming, basically anything to start moving and give yourself the message that you are going to be fit and happy. Dance videos can be found on the Internet through *Amazon.com*, in all the bookstores, and at big box stores like Target and Wal-Mart. *Livestrong.com* is a website with many diet and nutrition tips and plans also, as well as exercise and workout routines. They have calorie counter applications for smartphones to use on the go. They calculate your caloric need based on age, weight and activity level, and then keep track of not only calories but the ratio of protein, carbohydrates and fats you have ingested daily.

There's a variety of gizmos and gadgets that track programs as well. Wearable technology, such as Fitbit, has an array of tools that process what you burn in energy, and they can track what you consume. This is sometimes a real eye opener into what you are consuming.

Remember to focus on your outcome. *Visualization* is as important of a tool in getting fit as it is in reaching your other goals or purposes. Star athletes and Olympians utilize visualization, and they focus on picturing their next win, see themselves being handed the gold medal or earning the winning touchdown, and imagine receiving all the hoopla that follows. They picture and feel themselves running faster than before. They feel the muscles working better than before.

Picture yourself in your ideal shape. Maybe one you had when you were younger or thinner or just one that you think fits you. Then focus like crazy on this shape. Act as if you're already there, and become comfortable in your new shape. Don't buy clothes in your current size, as this is encouraging yourself to stay the same. In the book *The Secret,* you are encouraged to instead focus on the clothes that you will be buying in the size you are striving for. Also, pay attention to your diet to learn proper nutrition and to be a healthy weight. Don't focus on being "fat." It's not just about losing weight.

The Importance of Sleep

Sleep is also essential to overall functioning. When we don't get enough sleep, we are zapped of energy, irritable and tend not to think as well. Although some can get by on five to six hours of sleep per night, it is typically recommended that you strive for eight solid hours of uninterrupted sleep to allow your body full recovery from the day. If you don't allow yourself the sleep your body needs, it will come back to haunt you later in the form of fatigue, ill health, weight gain and any other number of problems that have been proven in studies. You'll notice your mood improves along with your ability to make better decisions with a full night's rest.

In your busy world, it may be hard at times to get the rest your body requires. Still, try to put forth a real effort to make your schedule fit this need. You would probably not go without bathing or eating for three or more days. Sleep is just as, if not more, important in terms of your overall health. It may be necessary to cut back on some activities or family outings if they are cutting into sleep time. However, the feeling of well-being that comes from getting enough sleep will override any temporary disappointment about rescheduling or removing an activity in your life.

If sleeping is difficult due to a snoring partner or outside noise, it may be helpful to sleep in separate rooms or to utilize earplugs and eyeshades. If only one partner likes to watch TV in bed, the other can purchase a headset to solve the problem. Make sure your room is dark enough and cool enough to allow for good sleep. Studies show that the body appears to like these environmental conditions for sleeping.

Tasks for Body Basics

Task #1 *Choose one of the healthy eating plans discussed within this Step and give it at least two weeks to a month to decide if you like how you are feeling.* If you don't care for it, choose another and also give that a couple of weeks to judge its effectiveness for you.

Task #2 *Choose a cardio exercise plan and do it at least a half hour daily.* Change it daily or weekly to reduce the chance of boredom.

Task #3 *Choose a resistance training or exercise plan that incorporates muscle toning with flexibility.* Build this in three times per week.

Get It Together

> *"The consequences of today are
> determined by the actions of the past.
> To change your future, alter your
> decisions today."*
>
> —UNKNOWN

This topic is important to the program for several reasons. Although it appears to be a mundane sort of thing, disorganization and the resulting chaos is one of the biggest problems reported by depressed and anxious individuals. It is also a problem for those with difficulty concentrating as well as those who experience trouble with boundaries and irritability. Organization is a critical topic. When disorganization is part of your normal, any sense of "calm" is quickly violated.

If organization isn't a problem for you (i.e., you feel in control of your house and work, paperwork and time management), you can skip this Step—and congratulations! That is one less thing you have to do!

The symptoms of feeling overwhelmed and not wanting to deal with the day often stem from not knowing where to start. Or you may not want to face the mountain of tasks that lie ahead. I have found some clients to be so bogged down that even the everyday task of leaving the house on time is too challenging. Their entire day is a mess before they ever get started and they are frazzled by 8 A.M. There are children screaming, pets needing a walk, work beginning at a certain time, the laundry isn't done, and available clothing is something picked out of the bin from the week before that didn't make it to the dry cleaner.

Stress chemicals are running rampant, and irritability and panic set in, as well as resentment of the household, job, family and whatever else. Does this sound like it could be your normal day? Who wouldn't be depressed?

Looking to outside sources to create inside solutions does not work.

Who wouldn't feel angry? This sets your whole day up to feel these negative emotions, as well as feeling anxiety-ridden. What's worse is that typically if disorganization is a problem at home, it's a problem at work as well. A cluttered desk, half-finished tasks, and unmet deadlines are the work version of the problem and are with you all day. Does your automobile look like a homeless person's shopping cart? If so, none of your major environments are peaceful. There is nothing pleasant about your surroundings and your internal stress meter shorts out.

The underlying emotion causing the distress is the feeling of not being in control. In fact, things feel totally out of control, and we then feel helpless in the face of the ongoing chaos. As we learned in the symptom section on Locus of Control, you may be looking for some outside source to take over for you, or you may be blaming some outside source or other individuals for your problems in this area. Remember, when you feel that things are outside your control, you feel depressed; despair can set in.

Looking to outside sources to create inside solutions *does not work.* The problem is *not* that you have too much to do or work full-time. It's that you haven't found *a routine and organizational plan* that works yet, or you found one but aren't consistent in following the plan.

Running around willy-nilly, being chronically late, never being able to find things, and having a dirty or sloppy house are stressful conditions and contribute to the anxiety-depression cycle. Things scattered about affect your ability to concentrate, and irritability sets in if not outright anger. Reflect on what your thoughts are while this is going on, keeping in mind the cognitive equation you learned of **T = PR** or **Thought = Physiological Response.**

Those thoughts probably sound something like this:

> *I will be late for work and get fired because it happens all the time.*
>
> *My children will be late for school and marked tardy for the fifth time.*
>
> *I can't find that project that needs to be in by 9 A.M.*
>
> *There are pages missing. The project needs to be in by 9 A.M.*
>
> *I'm going to have to eat fast food because I don't have time to make breakfast, and I am already twenty pounds overweight.*
>
> *I can't find my keys so I can't get to work.*
>
> *I can't even look at the sink because it's so full of dirty dishes.*
>
> *I have to go to the bank and can't find my paperwork.*
>
> *A check bounced because my checkbook is a mess and I don't know where the problem is. Now I have a forty-five dollar fee.*
>
> *The dog has a snarled hairball on his side the size of Rhode Island, and I don't have time to get him to the groomers.*
>
> *Whoops, I forgot to pick up the dog at the groomers.*

You get the picture. Not one of these thoughts brings about peace and serenity in your brain. They're alarming at best and exhausting at worst. Just think about if you have more than one of them each day, just in the first hour of waking up. Your physiological response to each of these involves your brain chemicals and the stress hormones, and you can see why you'd be off balance right from the get-go. Cortisol would be gobbling up serotonin at the speed of sound. The stress hormones would also cause your metabolism and digestion to get out of whack, further contributing to any weight problem you may also have.

I cannot stress to you enough the importance of this—being organized is peaceful. Being organized with your things and your time makes you more effective, more peaceful, more efficient and more successful in general. *Being organized feels good.*

Worth Learning and Doable

Look around your house. It should be your sanctuary, not a hell hole screaming your name to come clean it. Imagine looking for your car keys and there they are, always in the same spot. Laundry done, folded and ready to wear for the entire week. It is possible and it's just all in the planning. The house and time management issues are all about the planning and execution of a schedule and routine.

Remember, *you* are in control of these things—your time, your house, all of it. If something isn't getting done or is causing you distress in the household, it's because you haven't found the right system *for you.* The system doesn't have to be complicated or involve expensive organizational tools. It will take a bit of doing to get it in place, and it's very well worth the time spent doing it. Not everyone has to have the same system and the ones that work for one family will not work for another. Hopefully, you will find yours here.

Very simply, *a place for everything and everything in its place* is a good saying to live by, and I would like you to consider it another new mantra to embrace (along with breathing "in through the nose and out through the mouth").

Think of the simplicity of *a place for everything and everything in its place.* Yet, this is the biggest bugaboo I see, not knowing where you left your car keys, articles of clothing, sports equipment, checkbook, credit card, purse, wallet, glasses—you name it. I use to struggle with these same issues myself and I understand the level of distress that accompanies them. One day I found myself having to get dressed in the dry cleaner's parking lot because I had no clothes clean at home. I had forgotten to pick them up. Then there was the time I had to ask the grocery store to put my groceries aside till I got back with my checkbook that I had forgotten or lost for the moment. When getting ready to sell my car, I found a year-old half-bagel under my car seat that I recognized as being from a bagel shop in Michigan where I did my internship, and I realized there had to be a better way.

Issues of disorganization and a lack of time management are usually because you were not taught these skills. Or maybe your parents tried to teach you, but you may have felt it wasn't worth learning at the time. *It is worth learning.* These are not skills people are born with, although it seems like some people are just neater than others. Some have a higher tolerance for clutter and chaos than others. It usually comes down to what you are used to being around.

Better Thinking for Better Homes

To compound the problem of disorganization in your spaces, you often allow your emotional state to dictate these practical matters. You think things like ...

I'm so depressed; I don't care what the house looks like.

I'm so nervous that I can't concentrate.

I'm so ADD; I will never be able to organize myself.

If you use this reasoning, you're stuck and focusing on what you don't want. You already learned that those sorts of thoughts are a no-no within *Advanced Thinking Skills* in Step 4.

It really doesn't matter if you're depressed or anxious. Your house and time need streamlining, and with that will come a lessening of your symptoms. You'll feel an immediate shift, just stemming from the empowerment you're giving yourself and the taking control of your life. If you really are ADD, then organization and time management are the very set of skills that you require. For others, some of the excuses used may be because you have a small foot in the Lazy Department or you don't want to be bothered. The latest TV reality show may be more interesting than the sock drawer at the moment.

Examples of better thoughts are as follows:

I would love to look around and see clean counters where I can prepare dinner.

My bedroom is peaceful, and I can get away from all the hustle and bustle there.

I will experience less anxiety when I have gained control of my living space and time.

My home will be neat and tidy in two weeks, no matter how I feel.

Getting Started

To get started, take an inventory of the areas where you need organizing. Maybe there is just one area that's out of control, such as the laundry or the kitchen, or perhaps the entire place needs an overhaul. Either way, it can get done and not be overwhelming by breaking it down into sections and tasks. The major areas that cause disruption are your house, car, purse or wallet, finances and paperwork. It could just be time management and not organization that will benefit you.

I'm going to take you through a general plan that you can institute immediately. Then I'll give you more detailed resources for expert organizational advice for doing the overhaul once and for all. You're going to love it!

1. **Get out a pad of paper and look around.** Jot down room-by-room what the major problems are, such as laundry everywhere, kids' toys, paper clutter, etc. Where are the major stressors? Don't "fix" anything; just write down what you observe.

2. **Now go to where these items would ideally reside.** Is there enough room for them all to be put away at once? Do you need to get rid of some of it or do you need more space or better organization of it? Make a note on your sheet. If you have enough space, then it is probably more a problem of time management and routine. If there isn't enough space, you may be keeping too much stuff or just not have the proper storage solutions. You have to work with what you have. Dreaming of a bigger house or apartment is not a solution.

3. **If you don't have an appointment calendar,** please get one now. If you have a family, get a big one that everyone posts

on that is visible and accessible by all. Everyone needs to be involved.

If you live alone, a portable one will be fine. You may also have an electronic one—don't use it solely. The reality is that not all items sync with electronic devices and appointments can be overlooked. Your goal is to visually see where you are spending your time. Few realize how much is spent in areas that are never acknowledged.

4. **On your pad of paper,** list every activity for the week that has to be performed as well as how long it takes. For instance, work 9 to 5, travel time 30 minutes each way. That's nine hours of your day, plus how long it takes you to shower and get ready. Then there are ballet lessons for daughter, one hour plus travel time on Wednesdays only. Put everything down and then write them in pencil on your new calendar. This shows you where your free time is going to be.

5. **Dedicate some of that free time** to getting yourself together. It won't take that long, although it seems daunting right now.

6. **Remember** to keep some of that time free for exercise.

7. **List all chores that require travel,** such as grocery shopping and stops at the dry cleaner's. Can you do those on your way home from work? Saturday mornings? Can you do them all at once, in order to be more efficient, rather than making multiple trips? Decide on a good time and put that on your calendar also.

8. **Think through your morning routine.** This is usually where the day starts to go downhill. How much time do you need to get yourself ready? Pets? Kids? Breakfast? Organizing the house before you leave so as not to come

home to a mess that can make you feel depressed and
overwhelmed? If you have a family, I suggest getting up
two hours prior to when you need to leave or when they
need to be out the door. This gives you time to get ready,
get them up and ready, prepare and have breakfast as a
family, and still squeeze in a 30-minute walk or exercise
of some sort. In order to do all this, you will need to have
already planned the night before for things such as:

- Lunches

- Clothing

- Homework

- Projects of your own

- List of priorities for the day, knowing exactly where to
  focus your energies on any given day

- Gas in car

9. **Now think through your evening routine.** How do you
   get the above things done? Is there too much stuff going
   on in your evenings? Are the kids in too many activities
   or do you need help getting them around? Are you eating
   healthy food at night? Are you eating too late and not
   cleaning up because you're exhausted? This means you have
   to get up to dirty dishes, toys and items scattered everywhere, clothes on the floor—it's all downhill from there.

   Remember, you are in control of your schedule and your
   life, and sometimes too much is just too much. If you're a
   parent, you may be trying to provide a good quality of life
   by having many activities available for your family. However,
   it's not a good quality of life if you're depressed and agitated,
   the house is a mess, and you're eating at drive-thru fast
   food restaurants every night. Think about the memories

you're creating. If you're single, think about your own memories when you are older and reflecting on your life. Visions of you eating mystery foods from wrappers as you work late at your desk to finish things due to playing the online game *Angry Birds* or checking Facebook all day are not great for the memoir writing.

Tactics for Specific Areas

Now you know where the problem areas are and where your time may be being wasted. You are prepared to become organized and time savvy. Below are some general guidelines that will make a world of difference immediately if you put them to work for you.

House

1. **Keep dishes and plates put away all the time,** fill dishwasher after every meal.

2. **Do a good cleaning once a week.** If you're a parent, enlist the family, including children, to help especially in their own rooms. This shouldn't be a struggle, remember you are in charge as a parent. Choose a morning or evening, and no activities happen for your family until rooms are clean once per week.

   Use common sense regarding children and the usage of cleaning chemicals. Laundry goes in hampers nightly, either common ones in laundry room or private ones in bedrooms. Young children can pick up their toys and learn to make the bed. Many people feel guilty about making their children learn chores but there's nothing to feel guilty about. They are simply participating in the household and will have to run their own households someday. If they learn now, they will not have to struggle with these issues later.

   If you have the extra money, consider paying for a cleaning service for a few hours each week—it can create several extra hours to dedicate to items that bring you happiness and fulfillment.

3. **Keep money matters in one place,** as well as files for all your important papers and issues such as credit card information, taxes, medical, legal, travel, etc. It's ideal to be able to put your hands right on something the minute you want it. Keep copies of important things in a safe deposit box in your bank in case of fire or theft. A safe deposit box costs roughly $40 dollars a year. You don't have to have an expensive or large filing cabinet for your financial records; one of the cardboard banker boxes that you can buy at Office Depot or Staples is the right size for files. Also, those boxes are portable and can be stored in a closet.

4. **Remember,** *a place for everything and everything in its place.* It's really that simple.

5. **Go with a schedule for cleaning**—weekly, daily, monthly and seasonally–and stick to it.

Financial

To be in a financial mess is very depressing and anxiety-provoking. It also can damage relationships. If you're in a relationship, you and your partner may have very different styles of organizing finances. In any case, you have to take control of your finances. If a partner does all the financial recording and planning, still make sure you understand what's going on, what accounts you have, and whose name is on them. What happens if the other person dies or in the case of divorce or a breakup? There is never a reason in a partnership for each person not to be fully aware of shared finances. Or if you and your mate keep separate finances, that is fine; just be in control of yours and the ones that your name is on at all times.

Many do not learn about money as children or just have never made it a point to learn it as an adult; some even feel uncomfortable with talking about or handling it. Every day you have to pay for things. You have to eat and live somewhere. It takes money to do these things. Money takes care of us in old age and pays our bills now. Saying you're not good with money is like saying you're not comfortable with buttoning your clothes. Money is not mysterious or scary; you don't need to be a mathematician to be "good" with it. There are many excellent books and websites written on financial matters and I have included several of them in the Appendix section at the end of the book.

Learn to balance your checkbook and do it. An alternative is do it online or use online banking to keep track. You still have to know how much you have spent on credit cards and whether you will have enough to pay them off. Don't spend more than you make each month. Don't buy a house you can never pay for and that leaves you not having enough money for anything else. That too is depressing. It's better to rent or own a smaller house and have money left over for recreation and fun. If you're in a financial mess, just the very act of starting to take control of it will make you feel better. Find less expensive things to do for a while until your finances are manageable.

Car

Does your car look like you live in it? This too is very stressful and carries chaos from your home into your driving. You'll be more distracted and harried while driving if your car is a mess.

1. **Clean it out daily,** from anything you may have eaten, wrappers, coffee cups, etc.

2. **Wipe console** free of dust and grime with a wipe made for this to free your view of dirt.

3. **Take it to the car wash once a week,** if finances permit, or at least every other. Look for coupons for car washes in your area, or go on special discount days.

4. Each child riding in the car is responsible for keeping his or her own seat area neat.

5. Wipe fingerprints and dog nose prints off windows daily.

Purse/Wallet

Purses and wallets can be another war zone that traps you in disorganization. A purse may be filled with extra papers, bunched up money, cough drops, candy with dirt embedded in the wrapper, year-old receipts, hair items and cosmetics of varying ages including ancient ones. It may be a virtual dumping ground of things collected daily. Whether it's a purse, wallet or both that you're using, it's time to consider what really should be there.

Go through all purses and take out all junk. Vacuum them out with a hand vacuum if you have one or use the nozzle on a regular vacuum. Just wiping them out with a damp cloth works well also.

Men and women both need to check wallets and throw out all old movie tickets, coffee receipts and the business cards of people you will never be calling. Order your paper money in denominations and insert it neatly into the wallet. If the change part of your wallet is bursting at the seams, remove some of it and store it in a re-closable plastic bag or place it in a container of some sort designed for holding change. Don't just throw change into random drawers or compartments of the car where you'll have to deal with it again later. At some point, it helps just to take it to the bank and trade it in so you don't have to look at it anymore. Spend your change wherever you can to keep it to a minimum in your wallet or purse.

Buy a *Pouchee Purse* or similar item and fill it with your necessary items. Pouchees are a great concept. They are manageable-sized "purses" with pockets for organizing your cell phone, credit cards, lipsticks and money and a few extras like aspirin or cosmetics. If it doesn't fit in the Pouchee, then you probably don't need it. You then insert it into the purse you're going to use that day, and when changing purses, all you have to do is move this one item from purse to purse (instead of all your individual items). They come in fun colors and some can actually be used alone also. It's a great accessory item that is truly functional.

Time Management

Chances are you need some help in this department also. Taking on too much, as well as not being organized, definitely places you on the Road to Depression and being overwhelmed. There is only so much time and only one of you. In order to manage time effectively, you have to take control of it and yourself, and not allow things to get in your way. Prioritize what has to be done on any given day and do those things first. As mentioned before, figure out how much time you need in the morning to get around and then plan for it. You probably need more time than you are currently allowing, especially if you have children. Morning routines are important, as well as evening and bedtime.

Work routines are very important also. Studies have shown that significant amounts of time are wasted daily by excessive email and social media use. If you're checking your Facebook page all the time, you may not be getting your tasks done. Those tasks can build up, ready to cause you more stress. Set daily goals and priorities, and then finish them.

Plan to get everywhere 15 minutes early. Being late for appointments reflects badly on you. The person you're meeting either thinks you are disrespectful of his or her time or completely disorganized. And, being late adds to your stress meter—something you don't want.

Be Present in the Moment

Being present has to do with peace of mind. Some think of it as *mindfulness,* which has increased in popularity in the US. Mindfulness has its roots in Eastern Philosophy and Buddhism, although there's no necessary religious component to practicing it. Everyone can enjoy the benefits.

Mindfulness is the practice of becoming more fully aware of the present moment, nonjudgmentally and completely, rather than dwelling in the past or projecting into the future. Consider it as being in the "here and now." Mindfulness is typically achieved through meditation but it can be practiced through daily living.

Simply focusing on the present moment and quieting your inner dialogue can help you attain mindfulness. You may have a constant inner chatter going on that keeps you from enjoying or even noticing what's going on around you. The chatter typically involves the past or the future. It brings with it feelings of regret, worry and guilt, as well as any number of other distressing emotions. This is all to no avail as the past is done and you cannot predict the future. Typically this chatter is fraught with all the negative language you learned to eliminate in Step 2, *Cognitive-Based Work.* It also typically contains the themes of our fears, which we became aware of in Step 5, *Lose the Fear.* If you find yourself worrying about necessary daily tasks, you can see where the need to organize and plan is important. You don't have to worry about these matters. When you have a plan in place for them, it allows you to free up your valuable mind space.

Mindfulness is actually gaining respect as a therapeutic treatment, particularly when combined with Cognitive Therapy. It's being used for the treatment of anxiety disorders, depression, relationship and anger issues, sleep problems, eating disorders and stress management. It is also being utilized in the medical world with pain management and diseases that are thought to have a basis in stress.

You may believe that multitasking is a desirable ability. It is not. Study after study has shown that multitasking is not efficient and your performance actually declines when multitasking is used. More errors are made and burn out for individuals comes faster. Your brains are simply not designed to focus on two things at once that require your full concentration. The most ridiculous manifestation of this idea is the phenomenon of texting and driving. Reading emails while talking to clients or customers on the phone is also not a good idea for business; the distraction can be heard in your voice and the customer is offended.

Your self-esteem and integrity are caught up in how well you perform. Why not give yourself the best advantage by paying full attention? Slow down, do one thing at a time, and do it well. If you have time constraints, then give each task whatever time is available by prioritizing it and pay attention to only it during that time. You'll feel better and still get to everything. In fact, you will see an immediate increase in your productivity and the quality of work performed, whether it's a household chore or a business brief. Again, you will feel in control of your life and that feels good.

Also, it's important to be present in the moment while interacting with others. Nothing says "You're not that important to me" as staring at your smartphone or tablet while your partner, friend or child is trying to talk to you. You are altering your relationships with these individuals forever when you repeatedly do this— negatively affecting the integrity of your bond with your partner or friend, or your child's self-esteem. People need interaction, and if you won't be present and talk to them, they will find someone who will.

Resources for Get It Together

As stated before, this Step is just presenting general guidelines for gaining peace and control of your life. However, these guidelines will get you started and provide immediate results, as well as significant reduction in your symptoms of anxiety and/or depression.

Now I would like to share with you some really terrific resources in the arena of organization and time management. There are many more, but I believe all you need to know lies within the ones I've chosen. They are not in order of greatness; they are all good. If you simply do one or more of the following, a bit at a time, you will master your organization and time management, and never again feel that your life is so out of control. They can be found also in the Appendix.

1. ***Flylady.net*** This is a fun and resourceful free website and community with all you'll ever need to know about having your house in order. There are also great tips on time management, etc. The site is very good, especially if you're starting from scratch, as she emphasizes not getting bogged down with this stuff by breaking it into 15 minute segments. The website and its information are presented in an engaging, non-threatening manner that entices you to get on board quickly.

2. ***OrganizeYourselfOnline.com*** This is a paid membership site with the capability to enter personalized goals. You'll find rich resource content about goal setting and organizing everything in your life. Worthwhile tips are offered, and again the site does not get you bogged down.

3. ***The Complete Idiot's Guide to Organizing Your Life***
Although I dislike recommending a resource that implies someone is an idiot, I think this line of books is popular

enough now that no one takes it personally. *The Complete Idiot's Guide to Organizing Your Life* by Georgene Lockwood is a comprehensive resource and the only one you'll really need for getting organized. This is a book full of terrific information and strategies, and it addresses every topic in the line of organization that you may need.

4. ***The Complete Idiot's Guide to Managing Your Time***
This is another comprehensive resource. If you master Jeff Davidson's book, it is all you need. This one for time management.

5. ***Know Your Life: By Organizing It!*** This is essentially a workbook taking you through all the various things in your life and having you put them down in writing, as well as getting it together. If you complete James P. Litchko's book, your stuff will be all in place. It is not a tutorial, like the above resources, but more a tool for keeping your most important information at your fingertips.

6. ***The Present: The Gift That Makes You Happier and More Successful at Work and in Life, Today!*** Spencer Johnson's book explains the concept of being in the present, as we discussed under mindfulness.

Tasks for Get It Together

Task # 1 *Implement the ideas discussed in this Step immediately.* When you can bring order into your life, no matter how small it is, stress is reduced.

Task #2 *Using one of the resources mentioned, put an entire household organizational plan in place.* Give yourself enough time so that you don't become overwhelmed trying to do it all in two days.

Task #3 *Repeat the above task for time management, at home and at work.*

Task #4 *Carve out some time where you will interact with significant others in your life without the tablet or smartphone in your hands or even within eyesight.* Listen to them and pay attention to their concerns, ideas and thoughts. This is time spent investing in your relationships and the others around you. It is valuable time.

Afterword

My goal was to make the Dysfunction Interrupted program user-friendly, and I hope I have you excited about your future and practicing all your new skills. It will take a bit of time for it to become routine, but you'll get there very soon. When something feels good, it doesn't take long for us to get on board. It also may appear that I have over simplified matters, but that was my very intent.

By simplifying something it takes away the feeling that it is too large to overcome. Individuals who have spent many years trying to obtain relief from depression, anger problems, anxiety and all the rest often come to the conclusion that it is too difficult and overwhelming with too many theories and moving parts, such as different types of doctors and medications, inpatient and outpatient clinics, and different types of therapies. They then give up and feel worse than when they started.

There are only so many things that can go wrong and most of them can be corrected with your own brain and thoughts. There is no law that feeling good has to be a difficult or impossible goal. And, there is no law in mental health that states it has to be a long and complicated process. It has just evolved into that over the years and become the norm for most. One reason why I promote and believe in Positive Psychology is that it has taken the focus off what is wrong. Instead, it examines the strengths and what is "right" with you.

I know that some of the concepts from this program may be new or foreign to you. If you feel that you need a bit more help with the program, go to the website *PsychSkills.com* and email me your question or call about obtaining some personal coaching. I am invested in your success and want you to gain as much as you can from this program.

If you have been pleased with your results, please share that with others.

Visit the websites *PsychSkills.com* and *DysfunctionInterrupted.com*. There will be resources added at regular intervals to supplement the Dysfunction Interrupted program.

> **If you are feeling overwhelmed, get stuck or don't understand something, remember that coaching and answers to emailed questions are available at *DysfunctionInterrupted.com* or *PsychSkills.com*.**

About the Author

A PSYCHOLOGIST AND ENTREPRENEUR, Dr. Sherman has studied the human mind and motivation for 20 plus years, resulting in the desire to combine a mental health program with the keys to success. Dr. Sherman employs a view of treatment that focuses on what is right and not what is wrong. She has successfully worked with thousands of clients, helping them to feel better as well as achieve success, happiness and great relationships.

Dr. Sherman is founder of PsychSkills Institute, a company that specializes in personal development and psychology practice based in Fort Myers Florida. Depression, anxiety and anger problems are just a few of the difficulties treated. As a speaker, she is available to present at conferences for keynotes and workshops.

She enjoys golf, reading, travel and cooking and is actively involved in charitable organizations.

Raised in New Hampshire, she and her husband now live in Florida and New Hampshire. Although spending most of the year in Florida, she considers herself a New Englander, relishing every moment she is there.

Working with Dr. Sherman

Speaking Engagements and Workshops: Dr. Sherman would be delighted to participate in your wellness conference or to speak to your group. Her expertise is in sharing with others how to eliminate emotional baggage in order to find better relationships, enjoy more success and raise emotionally healthy children. If you want a highly interactive, informative and fun presentation or workshop, call her.

Her dynamic presentations include:

- *Dysfunction Interrupted: Don't Let Your Past Be Your Future*
- *Seeking Mr. Wrong-Understanding the 4 Major Reasons We End Up With the Wrong Men/Women and How to Pick the Right One*
- *New Relationships with Old Baggage-Are You Doomed?*
- *5 Reasons You May Still Be Depressed After Trying "Everything"*
- *9 Things You Can Do That Will Reinvent Your Life Right Now, No Matter What*
- *The "Advanced Thinking Skills" You May Not Know You Needed, But You Do*

Do you need coaching? Dr. Sherman works with a wide variety of clients who feel stuck in emotionally unsuccessful patterns such as depression and anxiety that cause them distress. Working together through the Dysfunction Interrupted methodology provides the professional support, information and mentoring you may need to overcome these dysfunctional patterns once and for all.

To determine if you would benefit from her expertise and involvement or to ask about availability for speaking at your conference or creating a workshop for your group, call or email.

Dr. Audrey Sherman
239-292-2451 | *ASherman@PsychSkills.com* | *PsychSkills.com*
DysfunctionInterrupted.com

 PsychSkills   **@PsychSkillsInst @DrAudreySherman**

 DrAudreySherman

Acknowledgments

I would like to thank everyone who has helped make this book possible. First and foremost I would like to thank all of my patients through the years for all of the experience and knowledge they have given me. It was because of them that I knew I needed to write a book and that it had to clarify all the mystery surrounding these emotional issues that cause such distress and waste their life. My hope was that writing this and laying it all out would save many more all the suffering and wasted time.

My writing needed a lot of help and I would like to next thank Judith Briles PhD, The Book Shepherd, for all of her assistance in the writing, publishing and marketing aspects of this project. There are a lot of moving parts and she "shepherded me" through all of them.

Rebecca Finkel did all the design work, inside and out, and I can't thank her enough for her patience and talent.

Finally, much gratitude goes to my husband Mike who made it possible for me to have the necessary time for this project.

Appendix: Further Exploration of the Topics

Family Styles and Dysfunction

Forward, Susan Ph.D., *Toxic Parents: Overcoming Their Hurtful Legacy and Reclaiming Your Life*. New York, NY: Bantam Books, 1989.

Neuharth, Dan Ph.D., *If You Had Controlling Parents: How to Make Peace With Your Past and Take Your Place in the World*. New York, NY: Cliff Street Books, 1998.

Schlessinger, Laura Ph.D., *Bad Childhood, Good Life: How To Blossom and Thrive In Spite of An Unhappy Childhood*. New York, NY: HarperCollins, 2006.

Young, Jeffrey, Ph.D. and Klosko, Janet, Ph.D., *Reinventing Your Life: The Breakthrough Program to End Negative Behavior and Feel Great Again*. New York, NY: Plume, 1993.

Anxiety and Anxiety Spectrum Disorders

Bassett, Lucinda, *From Panic to Power: Proven Techniques to Calm Your Anxieties, Conquer Your Fears and Put You In Control Of Your Life*. New York, NY: HarperCollins, 1996.

Bourne, Edmund Ph.D., *The Anxiety and Phobia Workbook*. Oakland, CA: New Harbinger, 2010.

Burns, David MD, *When Panic Attacks: The New Drug Free Anxiety Therapy That Can Change Your Life*. New York, NY: Morgan Books, 2007.

Klaus, William Eddy & Carson, Jon Speed., *The Cognitive Behavioral Workbook for Anxiety: A Step by Step program*. Oakland, CA: New Harbinger, 2008.

Pavilanis, Steve & Lee, Patricia, *A Life Less Anxious: Freedom From Panic Attacks and Social Anxiety Without Drugs or Therapy*. Chicago: Alpen Publishing, 2010.

Attachment

Clinton, Tim Ed.D & Sibcy, Gary Ph.D., *Attachments: Why you Love, Feel And Act The Way You Do*. Brentwood TN: Integrity Publishers, 2002.

Levine, Amir M.D., and Heller, Rachel, MA, *Attached.: The New Science of Adult Attachment And How It Can Help You Find-And Keep- Love*. New York, NY: Penguin Group, 2010.

Boundary Issues

Cloud, Henry, & Townsend, John, *Boundaries with Kids: How Healthy Choices Grow Healthy Children*. Grand Rapids, MI: Zondervan, 2001.

Cloud Henry & Townsend, John, *Boundaries: When to Say YES, When to Say NO, To Take Control of Your Life*. Grand Rapids, MI:Zondervan, 1992.

Cloud, Henry, *Necessary Endings: The Employees, Businesses and Relationships That All Of Us Have to Give Up in Order to Move Forward*. New York, NY: HarperCollins, 2010.

Hawkins, David, *Dealing With The Crazy Makers in Your Life: Setting Boundaries on Unhealthy Relationships*. Eugene, OR: Harvest House Publishers, 2007.

Caretaking and Codependency

Beattie, Melody, *Codependent No More: How To Stop Controlling Others and Start Caring For Yourself*. Center City, MN: Hazeldon, 1986.

Beattie, Melody, *The New Codependency: Help and Guidance for Today's Generation*. New York, NY: Simon & Schuster, 2009.

Hemfelt, Robert, Minirth, Frank & Meier, Paul, MD, *Love Is A Choice: the Definitive Book of Letting Go of Unhealthy Relationships*. Nashville, TN: Thomas Nelson, Inc., 2003.

Miller, Angelyn, *The Enabler: Why Helping Hurts the One You Love*. Tucson, AZ: Wheatmark, 2008.

Norwood, Robin, *Women Who Love Too Much*. New York, NY: Pocket Books, 1985.

Anger Issues

Goleman, Daniel, *Emotional Intelligence: 10th Anniversary Edition; Why It Matters More Than IQ*. New York, NY: Bantam Dell, 2005.

Harbin, Thomas, *Beyond Anger: A Guide for Men: How to Free Yourself From the Grip of Anger and Get More Out of Life*. New York, NY: Marlowe & Company, 2000.

McKay, Matthew and Rogers, Peter, *The Anger Control Workbook*. Oakland, CA: New Harbinger, 2000.

McKay, Matthew, Rogers, Peter and McKay, Judith, *When Anger Hurts: Quieting the Storm Within, 2nd Edition*. Oakland, CA: New Harbinger, 2003.

Depression

Burns, David, MD, *Feeling Good: The New Mood Therapy*. New York, NY: Avon, 1999.

Ilardi, Stephen, *The Depression Cure: The 6 Step Program to Beat Depression Without Drugs*. Cambridge, MA: DeCapo Press, 2010.

Knauss, William, *The Cognitive Behavioral Workbook For Depression*. Oakland, CA: New Harbinger, 2006.

Martin Seligman, *Authentic Happiness: Using the New Positive Psychology to Realize Your Potential for Lasting Fulfillment*. New York, NY: The Free Press, 2002.

Learned Helplessness and Locus of Control

Robbins, Tony, *Awaken the Giant Within: How to Take Immediate Control of Your Mental, Emotional, Physical & Financial Destiny!* New York, NY: Free Press, 1992.

Seligman, Martin, *Learned Optimism: How to Change Your Mind and Your Life*. New York, NY: Vintage Books, 2006.

Seligman, Martin, *What You Can Change and What You Can't: The Complete Guide to Successful Self Improvement*. New York, NY: Vintage Books, 2007.

Self Esteem

Engel, Beverly, *Healing Your Emotional Self: A Powerful Program to Help You Raise Your Self Esteem, Quiet Your Inner Critic, and Overcome Your Shame*. Hoboken, NJ: John Wiley & Sons, 2006.

McGraw, Phillip *Self Matters: Creating Your Life from the Inside Out*. New York, NY: Free Press, 2003.

McKay, Matthew & Fanning, Patrick, *Self-Esteem: A Proven Program of Cognitive Techniques for Assessing, Improving, and Maintaining Your Self-Esteem*. Oakland, CA: New Harbinger, 2000.

Schiraldi, Glenn, *10 Simple Solutions for Building Self-Esteem: How to End self-doubt, Gain Confidence, & Create A Positive Self-Image*. Oakland, CA: New Harbinger, 2007.

Personality Disorders

Goodman, Cynthia & Leff, Barbara, *The Everything Guide to Narcissistic Personality Disorder: Professional, Reassuring Advice for Coping with the Disorder-at work, at home, and in Your Family*. Avon, MA: F & W Media, Inc., 2012.

Kapuchinski, Stan, *Say Goodbye to Your PDI (Personality Disordered Individuals): Recognize People who Make You Miserable and Eliminate Them From Your Life-For Good!*. Deerfield Beach, FL: Health Communications, 2007.

Porr, Valerie, *Overcoming Borderline Personality Disorder: A Family Guide For Healing and Change*. New York, NY: Oxford University Press, 2010.

Roth, Kimberlee, Friedman, Freda & Kreger, Randi, *Surviving a Borderline Parent: How to Heal Your Childhood Wounds and Build Trust, Boundaries and Self Esteem*. Oakland, CA: New Harbinger, 2004.

Poor Coping Strategies

Albers, Susan, *50 Ways to Soothe Yourself Without Food*. Oakland, CA: New Harbinger, 2009.

Moran, Victoria, *Fat, Broke & Lonely No More!: Your Personal Solution to Overeating, Overspending, and Looking for Love in All the Wrong Places*. New York, NY: HarperCollins, 2007.

Pottle, Kim, *Numb No More: Simple Solutions to Achieve freedom from Habits and Addictions*.

Schaeffer, Brenda, *Is it Love or Is It Addiction: the Book That Changed the Way We Think About Romance and Intimacy*. Center City, MN: Hazeldon, 2009.

Relationships

Evans, Patricia, *The Verbally Abusive Relationship: How to Recognize it and How to Respond-2nd Edition*. Avon, MA: Adams Media Group, 1996.

McGraw, Phillip, *Relationship Rescue: A Seven-Step Strategy for Reconnecting With Your Partner*. New York, NY: Hyperion, 2000.

McKay, Matthew, Fanning, Patrick, & Paleg, Kim, *Couple Skills: Making Your Relationship Work*. Oakland, CA: New Harbinger, 2006.

Schlessinger, Laura, *Ten Stupid Things Couples Do to Mess Up Their Relationships*. New York, NY: HarperCollins, 2001.

Cognitive Based Work

Burns, David, MD, *Feeling Good: The New Mood Therapy*. New York, NY: Avon, 1999.

Goleman, Daniel, *Emotional Intelligence: 10th Anniversary Edition; Why It Matters More Than IQ*. New York, NY: Bantam Dell, 2005.

Robbins, Tony, *Awaken the Giant Within: How to Take Immediate Control of Your Mental, Emotional, Physical & Financial Destiny!* New York, NY: Free Press, 1992.

Seligman, Martin, Authentic *Happiness: Using the New Positive Psychology to Realize Your Potential for Lasting Fulfillment*. New York, NY: The Free Press, 2002.

Seligman, Martin, *Flourish: A Visionary New Understanding of Happiness and Well-being*. New York, NY: Free Press, 2011.

Seligman, Martin, *Learned Optimism: How to Change Your Mind and Your Life*. New York, NY: Vintage Books, 2006.

Biofeedback

Albright, Clare, *Neurofeedback: Transforming Your Life with Brain Biofeedback*. 2010

Swingle, Paul, *Biofeedback for the Brain: How Neurotherapy Effectively Treats Depression, ADHD, Autism, and More*. Piscataway, NJ: Rutgers University Press, 2008.

Association of Applied Psychophysiology and Biofeedback – *info@aapb.org*

Heartmath.com for EmWave products

Stresseraser.com for Helicor products

Wilddivine.com Home use meditation and breath training products

Advanced Thinking Skills

Byrne, Rhonda, *The Secret*. New York, NY: Atria Books, 2006

Hill, Napoleon, *Napoleon Hill's Keys to Success-The 17 Principles of Personal Achievement*, New York, NY: Penguin Books, 1997.

Hill, Napoleon, *Think & Grow Rich*, New York, NY: Random House Publishing, 1960.

McGraw, Phillip *Self Matters: Creating Your Life from the Inside Out*. New York, NY: Free Press, 2003.

Robbins, Tony, *Awaken the Giant Within: How to Take Immediate Control of Your Mental, Emotional, Physical & Financial Destiny!* New York, NY: Free Press, 1992.

Seligman, Martin, *Authentic Happiness: Using the New Positive Psychology to Realize Your Potential for Lasting Fulfillment.* New York, NY: The Free Press, 2002.

Seligman, Martin, *Flourish: A Visionary New Understanding of Happiness and Well-being.* New York, NY: Free Press, 2011. *authentichappiness.com*

Fear

Bassett, Lucinda, *From Panic to Power: Proven Techniques to Calm Your Anxieties, Conquer Your Fears and Put You In Control Of Your Life.* New York, NY: HarperCollins, 1996.

Hill, Napoleon, *Napoleon Hill's Keys to Success-The 17 Principles of Personal Achievement,* New York, NY: Penguin Books, 1997.

Jeffers, Susan, *Feel The Fear And Do It Anyway.* New York, NY: Ballantine Books, 1987.

McGraw, Phillip *Self Matters: Creating Your Life from the Inside Out.* New York, NY: Free Press, 2003.

Enrichment

Seligman, Martin, *Authentic Happiness: Using the New Positive Psychology to Realize Your Potential for Lasting Fulfillment.* New York, NY: The Free Press, 2002.

Seligman, Martin, *Flourish: A Visionary New Understanding of Happiness and Well-being.* New York, NY: Free Press, 2011.

Sher, Barbara, *Live The Life You Love.* New York, NY: Dell Publishing, 1996.

Body Basics

Cordain, Loren, *The Paleo Diet: Lose Weight and Get Healthy by Eating the Foods You Were Designed to Eat.* Hoboken, NJ: John Wiley & Sons, 2011.

Danzinger, Lucy, *The Drop 10 Diet: Add to Your Plate to Lose the Weight.* New York, NY: Ballantine Books, 2012.

Roizen, Michael & Oz, Mehmet, *You Losing Weight. The Owner's Manual To Simple and Healthy Weight Loss.* New York, NY: Free Press, 2011.

weightwatchers.com | *beachbody.com* | *Livestrong.com* | *thepaleodiet.com* | *self.com*

Getting It Together

Davidson, Jeff, *The Complete Idiot's Guide to Managing Your Time, 3rd Edition.* New York, NY: Penguin Books, 2002.

Johnson, Spencer, *The Present: The Gift That Makes You Happier and More Successful at Work and in Life, Today!* New York, NY: Doubleday, 2003.

Litchko, James, *Know Your Life: By Organizing It!* Annandale, VA: Tiny Kitchen Publishing, 2004.

Lockwood, Georgene, *The Complete Idiot's Guide to Organizing Your Life, 5th Edition.* New York, NY: Penguin Books, 2002.

Flylady.net | *Organizeyourselfonline.com*

Index